3 by 5

JOHN FITZGERALD KENNEDY

MAN OF COURAGE

To Hy,
CIVILIZED GENTLE MAN

John Fitzgerald Kennedy

MAN OF COURAGE

By Flora Strousse

ILLUSTRATED WITH PHOTOGRAPHS

American
Background
Books

P. J. Kenedy & Sons · *New York*

CONTENTS

NOTE TO THE READER:

In dramatizing this book, portions of the dialogue have been invented. This has been done with strict regard to factual material, taken from previous biographies.

F. S.

1

✫✫✫✫✫✫

WHEN JACK WAS YOUNG

JOHN FITZGERALD KENNEDY had learned many lessons during the first six years of his life. Perhaps the most important was that in the Kennedy family one did not stand still. Change was the keynote. For instance, though his name was really John, he was usually called "Jack," which had a more manly ring. Since this was so, he liked the sound of "Jack," because behaving like a man and being a good sport brought praise from his big brother and his father.

This meant standing up to brother Joe and fighting back, and not being a "cry baby" when he was bested, which he always was. Sometimes when his big brother hit him harder than he meant to and really hurt, Joe was sorry. Then when their father came home, Joe would give a good report.

"You know, that kid can really take it, Dad," he would say. "I knocked over his bicycle and he got konked on the head. But did he cry? Not one tear."

But then, neither had Joe cried when their mother gave him a whack on the seat for having treated his little brother too roughly.

It was funny about their mother. She was sweet and gentle and given to moments of calling him "my little John"—not "Jack." He and his mother had secrets. For one thing, she knew, and didn't think it so bad, that he sometimes wanted to cry, and even guessed the reason when he hid away to cry where no one could see.

He usually exchanged these secrets with his mother when the girls were asleep, upstairs in the comfortable three-story frame house in Brookline, Massachusetts. There was Rosemary, who had taken *his* place as the baby; then Kathleen had come along and taken *her* place, and then little Eunice had arrived and taken Kathleen's place. Nobody stayed THE BABY in their house very long.

So when you got a little sense and *should* know right from wrong, and didn't behave—which meant picking up food with your fingers, or telling fibs, or being impolite to grownups, or trying to get out of saying your prayers—you would get a sharp whack on the seat. It *was* funny. His mother never shouted, even when scolding, but she often said:

"Spare the rod and spoil the child." Though he did not quite understand what that meant, Jack knew it had something to do with a whack on the seat.

Anyhow, when his big brother Joe was sorry, he was wonderful. He would say, "You're a good scrappy kid, Jack. A real Kennedy. Just let any bully pick on you, and I'll show them."

Such words brought the same warm feeling as a

cup of hot chocolate on a wintry day. Everyone knew he loved chocolate more than any other flavor. And that time when Joe flipped over his bicycle, and he fell so hard he got a large bump on his head, his big brother had brought him a chocolate bar. At first he refused to take it. His head was hurting; he was good and angry.

"Oh, come on, Jack," Joe begged. "I bought it out of my allowance."

That really proved he was sorry. Joe always talked about how small his allowance was.

Let him be sorry! Jack wanted to be alone, so he could cry. So he just shook his head.

"It's great stuff. Smell," Joe insisted, waving the candy bar under his brother's nose. The smell was so sweet, so tempting. But he closed his lips real tight.

When he really got sore, and wouldn't, wouldn't, wouldn't, his mother called this "John's stubborn streak."

"Just like a mule," his father once stated.

"And where would he be getting a trait like that?" his mother had asked teasingly.

"From my side of the family," his father admitted. "But it's not a bad thing to hold to an idea when you think you're right, Rose."

And that time with the candy bar Jack *had* been right. Besides the bump on his head, he had minded because the fall scraped some of the paint off his brand-new bicycle. So even though his mouth was watering to clamp over the chocolate, he steadfastly refused. For a while, anyway. Later, after Joe had flung an arm around his shoulder and said he was really sorry, and then had peeled tinfoil off the candy bar, Jack had not been able to resist.

But before taking a bite, he offered the candy to his brother.

"You take half, Joe."

"Sure, if you want me to."

Briefly, they chewed in silence. Then Joe suddenly asked, "You aren't going to tattle?"

"Of course not."

"Great. Tell you what I'll do—I'll get some paint and touch up your bicycle."

"I'll help."

"Sure," said Joe.

"And," his big brother had added, "I'll save all the tinfoil I get for a week and give it to you. Then your ball will be big as mine."

This was something! From scraps of foil saved from candy bar and chewing gum wrappers, Joe had molded a great silver globe, bigger than a baseball.

"As big as yours?" Jack asked excitedly.

"Well, *almost.*"

Who would blab on a brother like that? But secrecy hadn't helped. As soon as they went into the house, their mother took one look at him and asked, "What happened to your head?"

"Oh, nothing."

"Don't tell me 'nothing.' I guess a hen flew up and laid an egg above your eye."

He touched the bump, winced, and said, "Oh, that—"

"Yes, that. How did it happen?"

Silence.

"Tell me," she insisted.

Joe spoke up then and confessed. He really had not meant to be so rough. He had just tipped the bicycle part way.

"I see," their mother said, and went to the kitchen for a cool plate, which she pressed against the bump "to take down the swelling."

After that, Joe got a whack on his seat.

It was about this time that young Jack learned his first lesson in logic. Before, he had halfway believed that when he was eight he would be as old and strong as Joe. Knowledge came suddenly that this would never be. When he was eight, Joe would be ten; when he was nine, Joe would be eleven, and so on until they were really old—like in their teens. So he would never be as big and strong as Joe. But then his father often said:

"Whatever you choose to do in life, boys, be the best."

He still had time to choose.

Never stand still. Change.

There had been many changes since May 29, 1917, when Jack was born. Only a month before that, behind his desk in the White House, President Wilson had known the sadness and responsibility of office. A man of peace, formerly a Princeton professor, he had hoped America would not become involved in war. But Europe, which had once seemed far away, had with faster ships come close. And huge German submarines skimmed beneath the surface of the seas like monstrous fish, ready to spit destruction at our shores.

After the sinking of the *Lusitania,* with the loss of 114 American lives, Germany had declared her intention of waging submarine warfare against ships of all nations. So America went to war, and her young men sailed off to foreign shores to "make the world safe for democracy." Those who remained put aside other tasks to throw themselves into the war effort. Jack's father was among them.

At the outbreak of the war Joseph Kennedy was twenty-nine years old, but he had already won a reputation as a good businessman. With the help of friends he had kept a small neighborhood bank, the Columbia Trust Company, from being taken over by a rival firm. He had earned the gratitude of the hard-working Irish families who deposited their money there and became the youngest bank president in Boston. When he joined the war effort, Grandpa Patrick Kennedy took over management of the bank.

Joseph Kennedy was proud of his new job as Assistant Manager of Bethlehem Shipbuilding Corporation's Fore River Shipyard at Quincy, Massachusetts. Surrounded by some of the biggest brains in the country, he listened, learned, and used every opportunity as another rung in the ladder toward success.

Of all the government officials he met none was so much admired by him as the vigorous, hard-hitting Assistant Secretary of the Navy, Franklin Delano Roosevelt. Temperamentally, the two had much in common, and Joseph Kennedy resolved that their paths should cross again in the future, if he had any say in the matter.

Once the war was over, he had joined the Boston

branch of Hayden-Stone Company, an important firm of investment bankers. Often away from home because of many duties, he frequently worked far into the night.

Sometimes when he was expected home for dinner, he phoned to say important matters had come up and he couldn't make it. Disappointed that he had been detained, Jack's mother would invite her father, John Fitzgerald, known in political circles as "Honey Fitz," to come share the meal. A former Mayor of Boston who had run for Governor the year before, Honey Fitz was a gay, high-spirited character, and it was for him Jack had been named.

While campaigning for the governorship, Honey Fitz had taken his namesake with him to tour the wards. Although Jack had been only five when he went on the stumping tour with Grandpa Fitz, age had been no barrier against the old man's showing the boy the art of political oratory. Jack had listened while coaxing words and flattery tripped from his grandfather's tongue, revealing the aptness of the nickname "Honey." With political rivals, though, he could be as peppery as relish and send an audience of old-time politicos into stitches by reciting in a brogue the well-known verse:

> And this is good old Boston,
> The home of the bean and the cod,
> Where the Lowells talk to the Cabots
> And the Cabots talk only to God.

If this wry toast tickled the fancy of his cronies, he still would not have recited it in his daughter's home.

Rose Kennedy would not put up with anything suggesting blasphemy, for she was a deeply religious woman. Indeed, her unswerving faith was the most steadying influence in a family made up of extreme individualists with up-and-down moods.

It was always fun when Grandfather Fitz was there, Jack thought, his nose pressed against the window to catch a first glimpse of the familiar figure. Why, he wondered, did people sometimes call his grandfather, "Little General"? He would have to ask him. But after they were all seated at the table, he forgot. Most of the talk was about the Red Sox, and their grandfather had brought along two beautiful, clean, white baseballs autographed by pitcher "Lefty" O'Doul.

In a voice shaking with excitement, Jack asked, "Is one for *me*?"

"Yep," Honey Fitz told him. "The players ask about *both* of my grandsons."

Imagine that! Those heroes remembering *him,* as well as Joe.

Grandfather Fitz had taken them both to the opening home game of the season, when the Red Sox played against the New York Yankees. Everyone in Boston must have been there, and everyone knew Grandpa Fitz. When the three of them came in, the band had struck up "Sweet Adeline" in honor of the ex-Mayor; this was his favorite song. People had whistled and sung almost as loud as they did a little later when a voice you couldn't see blared out "The Star-Spangled Banner." The only difference was that then everyone had stood at attention, and the flag was raised. Joe had known many more of the players' names than he: Collins, Harris, Shanks, McMillan, and millions more. Good thing, Jack thought, I remember well. Next time, *he* would know the names of the players, too!

At the dinner table brother Joe was speaking to him now.

"Let's see your ball, Jack," he said.

"Now, they're both the same," Grandfather Fitz put in, "except each has your own name on it."

"It was sure swell of you to bring them, Grandpa," Joe said. "Some day, I'm going to be on the Red Sox team."

"Me too," Jack echoed.

"Maybe," their mother said. "Meanwhile, watch yourself with those hard balls; I don't want any more lumps on heads in a hurry."

"We'll be careful, won't we, Jack?" Joe said.

Still almost speechless with pride and excitement, Jack mumbled, "Sure."

After dinner Grandpa Fitzgerald talked about the past. He told tall tales, mostly about himself, but he also praised their Grandfather Patrick Kennedy, saying how admirable it was for a self-educated man to have worked his way up to an important position in the State legislature and become so powerful a member of the Democratic Party.

"Yes, Patrick's a fine fellow," he said, "though we do have our differences." Then he went on boasting a bit about himself, which he claimed was any man's prerogative. He told with the same gusto as he had many times before, how in 1916 he had come within thirty thousand votes of Henry Cabot Lodge in the primary election for Senator.

"If I'd won," he added mischievously, "all the Boston blue bloods would have drowned themselves in the Bay."

Like their father, he joked about Boston society, but without bitterness. Generally speaking, he had got where he wanted and was known throughout the State, so why should he worry?

"As I always say," he went on, and he certainly always did, "I'd rather be a big fish in a small pond, than a small fish in a big pond, like some other people I know."

"If you mean Joe, never fear, he'll be a *big* fish in a *big* pond," their mother told him.

When she sighed, Honey Fitz said, "You don't look so happy about going up in the world."

"I'd be content not to move so fast," she admitted. Later, their mother played the piano and Honey Fitz sang, the boys joining in. It was such fun, and nobody scolded.

Finally, in bed, Jack felt as if he were floating on a cloud. The autographed baseball under his pillow, he soon fell asleep and dreamed he was pitching for the Red Sox. The umpire said, "One, two, three strikes; *you're out!*" Imagine, it was big brother Joe he struck out!

"You're a great scrappy kid. Here, have a bar of chocolate," sounded in his dream.

But as he was about to take a bite, a real voice floated from downstairs. His father had come home, and he was talking about some of the things that had happened during the war.

"And I told Franklin Roosevelt," he was saying, "that Bethlehem ships would not be delivered to the Argentine until all the bills for their construction had been paid for. He gave me a pep talk about war effort, but I held my ground. So what do you suppose he did?"

"What?" Honey Fitz asked.

"He sent the Navy up the Fore River and tugged the ships away."

Suddenly, instead of being angry, his father burst out laughing—loudly.

"Come to think of it," he said, "I would have done the same. That Brass Hat has plenty of brass; he'll be going places, mark my word. And if I keep my wits about me, maybe I'll be going there with him."

"It's always go, go, go around here," his mother said. "But that's the way you want it."

His father's voice sounded anxious when he asked, "Isn't that the way *you* want it, Rose?"

"I could be content with what we have," she told him. "But where you go, I go."

"There's an old saying about the 'best laid plans,' " Grandfather Fitz reminded.

"True," Jack's father said. "But there are many ways of getting ahead, and I know all of them."

"That you do, my lad," Honey Fitz agreed. "And though Boston will always be good enough for me, I'm sure you'll be making a great name for yourself beyond—besides, it can't be denied you've made my daughter happy."

"Imagine his admitting that, Rose," his father said. "Yes, imagine!"

They both laughed, and started to tease Grandfather Fitz.

"If you don't be stopping now, I'll sing 'Sweet Adeline,'" he warned.

Jack couldn't remember if that was a song or not, because as soon as he touched the baseball again he fell asleep.

2

✫✫✫✫✫✫

BOYHOOD IN BOSTON

ONE THING young Jack couldn't be quite certain about was whether their houses got bigger because there were more babies, or whether there were more babies because their houses got bigger. Anyway, both happened: more babies and bigger houses.

Their new home was huge, with a long porch running halfway around it and great shade trees rising above the lawn. Now there was plenty of room for the boys to race and romp. And indoors they discovered the magic of fireplaces. As they sprawled on the floor in front of the hearth with their books, the sound of flames fanning upward and the shadows they cast across the pages made stories seem more real.

One of Honey Fitz's favorite pastimes was recalling the time when he was young and had listened to literary conversations at the Old Corner Bookstore. Like old landmarks visited with their mother—Plymouth Rock, Concord Bridge and Bunker Hill—the names of Ralph Waldo Emerson, Henry Wadsworth Longfellow and James Russell Lowell came to have a familiar ring to the boys.

When Jack ran across words that were unfamiliar or too long, he would fill in with his own—for if care slowed up curiosity, care must go. Thus, though he was to be an avid reader, Jack's spelling for many years was reported as "atrocious." Joe could read faster than he and knew more words, but he couldn't stay still as long. So, often before Jack had finished his story, his big brother would say:

"Let's go out and get some air—play tag—have a catch."

Usually he would agree, because if he didn't, Joe would whistle and tease so that he couldn't read anyway. At least, that was how it used to be, until something happened.

Joseph Kennedy was away now as much as he had been during and after the war. As Honey Fitz had predicted, his son-in-law was "going places beyond" —beyond Boston—and at even a faster rate than he himself could have hoped for. Business often kept him in New York.

But on this particular day, Joseph was home with the family. Very pleased he was, their father said, with the way the girls were growing. But his chief interest was watching the boys. Because of his attention, the "something happened" that pleased Jack very much and helped the boy decide he didn't *al-*

ways have to put down his book the second Joe told him to.

It was Sunday. Snow had been falling for the past few days and all the world was white. Stiff, bleak branches on their shade tree were now rounded blobs of beautiful whipped cream. Jack gazed out the window.

Far off, near the hedge, was the sagging fortress he and Joe had built before pelting one another with icy snowballs at the "Battle of Bunker Hill." Close to the house was their snowman, whose smile at first had looked like Grandfather Fitz's. Since the weather had turned warmer, though, he had melted thin and his lips were a straight line; now he looked like Grandpa Patrick.

Jack turned from the window. It was a dreary day, but here in the large living room, this didn't matter. A log cracked; flames hissed on the hearth and sent shivering shadow vines to clamber up a wall.

On the way home from Mass, his mother had said, "If it doesn't clear up, I don't think I'll let the boys visit Father Patrick this afternoon."

"You mustn't coddle them," their father said.

" 'Coddle!' They've been practically rolling around in snow since it started. And Jack—sometimes I don't know what gets into him. You'd think it was summer the way he runs around. What he's got against hats and heavy coats, I can't imagine."

"Maybe he thinks that mop of hair is a hat," young Joe put in.

This was a touchy subject. Jack had enough trouble

keeping his bushy forelocks slicked down without being reminded of the problem.

"It's better than being bald," he returned.

"Who's bald?" his brother asked.

"Well, maybe you aren't yet, but just wait . . ."

Their father cut in, saying that if they had to argue, it should be about something more worthwhile. He would decide later whether to take them to Grandfather Patrick's and in the meantime they should occupy themselves.

Their mother had gone upstairs to tend Rosemary, whose cough had developed into "croup"; their father was in his study on the second floor, "getting some letters out"; brother Joe had disappeared, and, from the scuffling sounds above, must be teaching little sister Kathleen how to kick a ball.

Jack decided to read his *Billy Whiskers* book.

The flickering light became a sea on which he sailed away to the Canary Isles. The ship his fancy chose for this long voyage was a swan boat like those in Boston Park. With Grandpa Fitz, he had often skimmed the lake in one of those great birds.

Anyway, now he was skipper of the swan boat, and steered his craft to the Canary Isles. There, the flapping of wings, bird song and the beat of tom-toms so filled his ears that a real sound in the room made him start.

"You sure read a lot for a little tyke," his father was saying, in tones that showered praise upon his head.

"Yes, I like to read," he said.

Joe came in and their father told him to sit down. He had been meaning to have a talk with them both, and this was as good a time as any. He asked about school, and Joe said he liked Dexter fine.

"Why?" their father asked.

When you said something, he always wanted to know the reason.

"Well," Joe told him, "the boys are polite, and they're also keen on sports. But sometimes it's hard to keep up with them."

"If you think of yourself as a winner and keep your eye on the goal, you'll probably make the grade," their father said.

"You can't always win," Jack said. "Like when I fight with Joe. And Grandfather Fitz—he lost the election."

"True," their father agreed. "Sometimes the odds are against you. Grandfather Fitz was a good Mayor, and would have made a fine Governor of Massachusetts. But those stuffed shirts on the Hill don't vote for men, they vote for the old first families."

He turned to Joe. "You show those boys in school what a Kennedy can do."

"I will," Joe said. "I will."

His brother looked so strong and manly, Jack was proud of him.

"Joe will," he put in.

He was rewarded by having his hair mussed up and hearing his brother say, "And Jack will show 'em, too. He's a good fighter, even if I usually beat him."

"I'm sure he puts up a good fight," their father said.

"But remember, both of you, to really move along; you've got to have something in your heads, so I expect you to study."

After they had promised they would, their father gave Jack a friendly wallop on the back and said, "It pleases me to see you so interested in books, son."

This praise and encouragement was what made him decide he wasn't going to stop reading the minute Joe told him to.

"This is a neat book," he said. "Say, Dad, where are the Canary Isles? I read about them in *Billy Whiskers*."

"Blamed if I know exactly," his father said. "So you see what happens if you don't pay attention to your studies."

Not quite able to accept that their father didn't know *everything*, Joe said, "But you *did* make the Harvard baseball team."

"That I did," he replied. "And even if Professor Holcombe did flunk me in Banking and Finance, there's little I don't know about those subjects now." He paused for a moment, then added, "That's not to say I shouldn't have studied harder, because I missed out on many things. So go get the atlas, Jack, and we'll look up the Canary Isles."

Late that afternoon the boys went with their father to Grandfather Pat's, and their mother made Jack wear a knitted cap and heavy jacket. Wait till he grew up; he would never wear a topcoat or a hat!

Grandfather Patrick was glad to see them, but when Jack tried to tell him how, after their snowman began melting, he looked like him, the old man was displeased. He looked even more like the snowman then, but Jack said he was sorry.

"I'm sure you didn't mean any disrespect," Grandfather said. "But there's a lot I want to ask your father, so you boys sit still and listen."

They tried not to fidget while their father told about all the important men he had met in New York. In the brokerage business he had learned a lot about investments, their father said, and was forming a syndicate to buy a chain of movie houses in New England.

"But Boston's not for me," he said. "It's narrow and bigoted. As soon as I see my way clear, I'm going to move the whole family down to New York."

Imagine that! Jack glanced at Joe, who also seemed surprised. Neither of them spoke, but Joe winked.

"I told you before, I don't like winking, Joe," Grandfather put in sharply.

As their mother often said, some people seemed to have eyes in the back of their heads.

"I'm sorry, Grandfather. I won't do it again," Joe promised.

Later, after they had gone home and were having dinner, Joe mentioned the business about moving. Their mother threw up her hands and said, "Not to New York! Is that on your mind, Joseph?"

Not for the present, their father told her. But if business kept him mostly there, it would only make sense to move.

"You wouldn't mind, if we were all together more, would you?" he asked.

Nothing would please her better than having him home more, their mother said. Still, she had so many friendly ties in Boston.

"Well, there's no use worrying about what won't happen for a while," he told her. "And, Rose, you can make friends anywhere."

That their father was well on his way toward making his first million would have meant little to the boys because, though they now lived in an expensive section of Brookline and had a staff of servants to maintain the place, they did not think of their surroundings in terms of cost. Their parents had made it a rule never to speak about money in the house, and never gave the children bigger allowances than those of the neighborhood youngsters.

Later, when Jack became a Boy Scout, he found he had to make a plea to his father for extra pocket money. His letter, though showing tact and reasonableness, fully confirms a blithe disinterest in grammar and spelling. He wrote:

My recent allowance is 40¢. This I used for aeroplanes and other playthings of childhood but now I am a scout and I put away childish things. Before I would spend 20¢ of my 40¢ in five minutes I would have empty pockets and nothing to gain and 20¢ to lose. When I am a scout I will have to buy canteens, haversacks, blankets, searchlights, poncho things that will last for years and I can always use it while I can't use chocolate marshamallow sundae ice cream and so I put in my plea for a raise of 30¢

for me to buy schut things and pay my own way around.

Finis,

JOHN FITZGERALD FRANCIS KENNEDY

Jack might have thought his father could not afford this increase! Perhaps the youngsters were equally innocent about money in other areas. Since Joseph Kennedy never discussed his fortune in front of the children, their father's "making good" must in their minds have seemed more like winning a game or an argument. They must also have felt success was somehow related to keeping on the move, because that was what their father did—go, go, go.

Before the family moved to New York, to a bigger, better house, there were more babies—Patricia and Bobby. Joe particularly welcomed another boy. He had said in disgust when Pat was born, "Four girls! If this keeps up, we'll have a petticoat football team."

"Why not?" their father asked. "It's as important for girls to be physically fit as boys."

Rosemary, who was shy and delicate, rarely joined their games. But when Kathleen booted a ball, boy! it went. So they nicknamed her "Kick."

When plans for moving were definite, their father told them about the fine new house and the lawn in Riverdale, the New York suburb, where they really could have a team.

"I'm sure you'll be happy there, too, Rose," he said.

"You don't have to build it up for me," she told him. "When you didn't get home for seven weeks at a time,

I made up my mind it was high time for us to join you."

"That's my girl!" their father said lovingly, and she blushed with pleasure.

3

✭✭✭✭✭✭

SCHOOL DAYS

LISTENING TO the clickety-clack of the wheels on the train rushing toward New York, Rosemary watched the landscape fly backward. The eldest daughter, she was a shy, quiet child who did not share her younger sister's competitive spirits. Joe and Jack, having been restrained from doing handsprings in the aisle, had started a pretended game of touch football in which Kathleen had also become involved. From her seat on the sidelines, Eunice confusedly called the plays, annoyed because the nurse would not allow her to join the skirmish.

Since this was their first long trip, the youngsters may well have imagined that all travelers on their train had the same sort of private car as the one provided for their family. Traveling with them was a staff of loyal help who wished to continue to serve the Kennedys in their new home.

Gazing up and down the car, Rose Kennedy thought

that her children had been blessed with rare good looks. Hurriedly, she corrected her wave of pride by silently adding, "Beauty is as beauty does."

Thoughtful, but resigned now to leaving old friends and relatives, she wondered if her husband would be at home with the family more than he had before. True, his business headquarters were in New York, where as a lone wolf he was now considered a "wizard" on Wall Street.

Restless, though, Joseph Kennedy had a "finger in every pie" and was constantly on the move to look after his many interests. He was here, there, everywhere—even as far as Hollywood, where he was in the process of buying one of the less well-known moving-picture companies. Still, she thought, his drive toward even greater success was, at least in part, to provide opportunities for the children.

Suddenly she became aware of the shouts of the boys as Jack raced toward the "goal line" with Joe and Kathleen in pursuit. Their mother insisted they calm down so that Pat and baby Bobby could take a nap.

This wasn't the way people behaved in trains, she told them, which they saw clearly when their own slowed up at a station. Through car windows on the other track they could see people seated quietly, reading or talking. Then, as the other train moved northward, the dining car came into view. People sat at tables, eating or being served by white-coated waiters.

Before anyone could speak, their mother said: "I know—you're hungry. All you need is the sight of food to make you so."

They agreed in chorus, and she pressed a small button alongside her seat. The porter appeared, and, after she told him they would like lunch, he disappeared again. He returned shortly with a smiling man who was wearing a white chef's cap. He brought in menus, which he read. After taking orders for Kathleen and Eunice, he asked what the others wanted.

"You and Jack take your time," their mother told the boys. And she gave them each a menu.

There were so many items, it was hard to make up one's mind. Besides, some of the words were foreign and hard to read, so Jack tried to remember the foods his mother had mentioned. First on his mind was last on the list: desserts. Pies, pudding, Jello, ice cream—a *chocolate nut sundae!*

"That's what I'll have," he blurted out.

"What?" Joe asked.

"Chocolate nut sundae."

"What—first, silly?" Joe said. To make matters worse, he added, "Can you imagine anybody who eats so many sweets being so skinny?"

"That's enough, Joe," their mother put in. "What will you have first, Jack?"

"Chicken," he told her. "Southern fried chicken."

"I can't imagine its being very 'Southern' here in New England," his mother said.

The man in the chef's cap assured her the chicken was very good, but if there was anything they wanted that was not on the menu, he could have it cooked to order.

"No indeed!" their mother exclaimed. "The choice

is excellent. We just need a little time to make up our minds."

"Of course," the man said. "Meanwhile, I'll see what the others want."

He then took the orders of the staff. When he returned, Jack stuck to his guns—he would take what he had said he would. But even the idea of food didn't keep him from fuming inside. After the man had hurried to a car in the rear, he turned to Joe, red-faced, and sputtered:

"You know what you are? You're a—a regular Benedict."

"A *what*?" his brother asked. "What's got into you?"

Jack warmed to his subject. "—No better than that sneak who sold our secrets to the British."

"*Him!*" Joe shouted. "Don't you call me a Benedict Arnold."

His anger was so genuine, his tone so threatening that Jack was almost tempted to retreat. He didn't, though, but instead explained the justice of his stand.

"You didn't have to call me 'skinny' in front of a stranger, did you?" he demanded. "That's like going over to the other team."

"Maybe you have a point," his brother conceded. "But take back calling me a Benedict Arnold."

"First, you take back calling me 'skinny' in front of a stranger," Jack said.

"Maybe I should have waited until he went," Joe said. "But you *are* skinny. Anyhow, take back what you said."

"O.K., I do—but watch your manners."

This phrase, lifted from their mother's vocabulary,

struck Joe as funny. He burst out laughing and said, "You're a card, Jack, but I'm on your side, honest." ·

"I knew it all the time," Jack told him, and he laughed too.

Jack was nine years old when the family moved to Riverdale. He entered the Riverdale Country School and remained there through the sixth grade, although in the meantime the Kennedys moved to nearby Bronxville, into a beautiful white house surrounded by big grounds. Jean, the youngest of the Kennedy girls, was born around this time, and Ted, the third Kennedy son, a few years later.

At the age of thirteen, Jack transferred to the Canterbury School in New Milford, Connecticut. Separated from his family for the first time, he kept a stiff upper lip about reactions that might have been considered "unmanly," until he had conquered them. Only after he was able to admit weakness in the past tense, did he write home:

> It's a pretty good place but I was pretty homesick the first night. . . . The swimming pool is great even though the football team looks pretty bad. You have a whole lot of religion and studies are pretty hard. . . . This place is freezing at night and pretty cold in the daytime. The food is pretty good better than you get in most schools. . . . I got the suit the other day but I did not like the color and it was pretty itchy looking material. . . .

Despite this lack of enthusiasm, letters followed that contained news aimed at pleasing his parents. To his mother, he wrote:

We have chapel every morning and evening, and
I will be quite pius when I get home.

For his father's satisfaction, Jack told of his sports
activities, football and baseball, which he played with
some success. It was in swimming, though, that he
made his greatest drives. It was the one activity in
which he would later excel his brother Joe, and that
one day would serve to cast Jack himself into a hero's
role.

Meanwhile, he used exploits of the gridiron to
sharpen a latent gift for drama and words, as when
he wrote:

We played Gunnery on Friday and much to my
surprise I played quarterback for the whole game
except three minutes. They licked us 32-0 they
smeared us and the score felt like it.

One fellow was running for a touchdown, and I
made a flying tackle and landed him. Everybody
said I played a good game . . . one of the fellows
was seventeen and when he hit you you stayed
hit. One time I got him out and what a pleasure it
was to see him roll and writher on the ground.

. . . And it was not a Sunday School picnic. You
would run through their line somebody would
whack you across the face somebody else would
crack your head. You would stagger, five fellows
would jump on your neck. They would get you
down. Then the six remaining fellows would sit on
you for all sorts of reasons each one had his own
particular desire. . . .

Even in fancy, though, he could not glorify his

scholastic grades. He did, however, make an effort to explain what must have been puzzling, even to himself. In later life John Fitzgerald Kennedy staggered all of his associates by almost total recall of correspondence, conversations and historical fact, while at the same time he blithely forgot to keep track of such sundry possessions as clothing, typescripts, memos and books.

Many gifted people retain vividly what strikes a core of interest and dismiss all else as unimportant. It is therefore highly possible that young Jack's difficulty with Latin was simply that he found the subject dull. This, though, would have been small comfort to a father for whom subtle reasons would only be "alibiing for not doing one's best."

Around this time Jack wrote in a letter home:

> . . . And though I may not be able to remember material things such as tickets, gloves and so on I can remember things like Ivanhoe and the last time we had an exam on it I got 98.

Jack's line of thought did little to make his father understand why, if a boy could get good marks in some grades, he had to fail in others. Joseph Kennedy stated this view in no uncertain terms. After the parental pep talk, Jack wrote, "My Latin has gone up thirteen points." His father's pleasure in this improvement must have grown even greater when his son wrote soon afterwards:

> Please send me Litary Digest. . . . I did not

know about the Market Slump until a long time after, or a paper. Please send me some golf balls.

What more was needed, his father thought, to prove Jack could do well with a little extra application? And it was good that the boy was taking an interest in current affairs.

He would tell his son that he was pleased, when Jack came home for Easter vacation. But he would also have to hammer at the theme of discipline.

Instead of lectures, though, Jack became the object of concern and tenderness. He was stricken with an acute attack of appendicitis, which prevented his return to Canterbury for the spring semester.

One day while he was still convalescing, his father broached the subject of changing schools.

"How would you feel about joining Joe at Choate?" he asked.

"Why don't you, Jack?" his brother urged. "Choate is the best prep school in the country."

Jack hesitated. He knew he would again be in competition with his big brother and would be forced to measure himself against superiority.

"What's wrong with Canterbury?" he demanded.

"I'd prefer you to go to Choate," his father said.

"Great," Joe said, as if it had already been decided. "I'll have another rooter in the cheering section."

"What a swelled head!" Jack said.

"We'll all be cheering for Jack, too, if he applies himself," their father put in.

"I'll try," Jack told his father.

And he would.

If Jack had been graded on the subjects which he enjoyed, his marks at Choate would have been very good indeed. His inattentiveness to studies that had no appeal was not willful, because there was nothing he wished more than to please his father. At this point, though, he seemed unable to turn away from activities pleasing to himself. Among these was the fun of finding new friends.

He knew that Joe could be depended upon in a crisis, and that the two would always stick up for one another. But Joe was very popular—the pride of professors and coach alike—and at Choate one did not bask in reflected glory.

Some of Jack's teachers might have thought of him as lazy, but this would have been hotly denied by others. Even if his spelling was still "atrocious," he made high grades in English because he showed a sense of drama and vividness in telling a tale. His interest in history and fairly avid reading of *The New York Times* would later serve to make him a keen student of man's past and present accomplishments. Indeed, his ability to memorize whatever he found appealing—plus a gift of gab on these subjects—evoked high praise from his friend LeMoyne Billings, when later he was asked to recall those early days at Choate.

"Jack was one of the most versatile people I had ever seen," Lem said. "Whenever anything was going on, he was in on it."

This estimate would have been of little comfort to Jack's father at the time, because whatever his son had been "in on" reflected little to be proud of on his report card.

Besides, Lem's views about his buddy must have been influenced by the fact that he, Jack and Rip Horton engaged in mischievous activities much frowned upon at Choate. They probably fancied themselves junior editions of the Three Musketeers, hands ever ready on the hilt to do battle against injustices by authority.

This carefree trio gave themselves the somewhat boisterous title of The Muckers, though the origin and meaning of this name remained obscure. The reported activities of The Muckers had the flavor of scattering spice. Most affected by their peppery mischief was the housemaster, J. J. Maher, who showed much patience as the victim of their boyish pranks.

A strict adherence to the schedule set down at Choate should have left little time for getting into trouble. The gong sounded at seven-thirty, which was the signal to waken, wash up, straighten the room and hurry to breakfast. This was followed by classes until three—with time out for lunch—and then came compulsory athletics until five. There was another round of wash-up before dinner and then chapel at seven-thirty. After that, the boys returned to their rooms to study until "lights-out" at nine-thirty. At specified times, each student was responsible for a thorough cleaning of his own room and waiting on tables. In spite of this orderly program, The Muckers found loopholes in the letter of the law.

The Muckers acted more in the spirit of fun than of deliberate disobedience. Food seemed to have played an important part in their escapades and their reasons for sneaking away after "lights-out" usually dealt with a trek to the village candy shop or Wallingford Inn. There they would disregard the menu and dive into pies, waffles, sundaes, banana splits, and chocolate.

The Muckers' reputation for fun acted as a lure for other hungry, restless fellows to gather in their rooms. As charter members, however, Horton, Billings and Kennedy were branded the ringleaders in the revolt against authority.

The housemaster, Mr. Maher, must have often been at wits' end coping with their mischief. Perhaps it was in the hope of curbing illegal exits from a window that the housemaster's wife frequently invited students to her apartment on Sunday evenings, for a batch of her famous waffles.

Her husband was also the football coach, and to enforce discipline did not hesitate to chasten the boys with a paddle. Many years later, when John Fitzgerald Kennedy returned to Choate, he reportedly said to his old coach: "You never could catch me with that paddle, could you?"

When John, as a famous man, ragged his old coach about not having been able to catch him, it was to put him at ease. The housemaster admitted that he never made contact between the paddle and Jack's rear.

Recalling those early days, Mr. Maher said, "You take Joe, he was a real athlete. But Jack made up for what he lacked in athletic ability with his fight. Jack was lazy in practice but not when the chips were down. When I tried to speed up football signal drills by running along behind the boys, I never could catch him. He'd lope along and when I'd get close to him he'd put on an extra burst of speed and leave me behind. He was terribly fast. I could run a hundred yards in eleven seconds, but he could beat me."

That Mr. Maher was a patient man in the face of boyish pranks can be seen by the tone of a series of letters he penned to Jack's father. Concerning some other weaknesses of the second Kennedy son, he wrote:

> Jack, I feel sure, is trying to be a better fellow, but at times the old habits are stronger than the new desire. He has been pretty consistently on time, and he has made an effort to be neat about his room—failures in that respect may be attributed to the fact that he has little idea of neatness. . . . But Jack is trying. And I'm sure his health is actually better for the lift even this little purposefulness has given him.

Later, the housemaster wrote in more despondent tones:

> I'd like to take the responsibility for Jack's constant lack of neatness about his room and person, since he lived with me. But in the matter of neatness, despite a genuine effort on Jack's part, I must confess failure. . . . Occasionally, we did manage to effect a housecleaning, but it necessitated my "dumping" everything in the room into a pile in the middle of the floor. Jack's room has throughout the year been subject to instant and unannounced inspection—it was the only way to maintain a semblance of neatness, for Jack's room was a club for his friends.

Little appreciating his housemaster's efforts in his behalf and his own father's growing impatience, Jack wrote home:

Things are going pretty well up here. We are upon Mr. Maher's corridor, right next to him, and everything we say, he bobs in and adds his comments. We are practically rooming with him, which is more than we bargained for.

Nor had he probably "bargained for" what happened shortly.

Usually after chapel the students returned to their rooms to study. This evening, though, something special must have been planned because they had not been dismissed. Jack stole a glance at his two friends, whose dark suits and polite expressions seemed to belie the fact that the three of them had gotten into trouble again last night.

After all, they had simply been acting out a historic event, the Battle of Bunker Hill, piling their bed-clothes into a mound to make the scene more realistic. They had not counted on two of the pillows' ripping, which had given a beautiful effect of snow and formed a slippery mat for them to slide on. When one of them fell to the floor with a thud, Mr. Maher had come in. J. J. was really sore this time! Pained, and with a kind of desperation, he had said:

"I've had enough. Clean up this mess and get to bed."

He then turned to Jack and said sternly, "And you—I regard your lack of neatness as quite symbolic—

aside from the value it has in itself. You are disorderly in almost all your organized projects. You study at the last minute, keep appointments late, have little sense of material values, and can seldom locate your possessions."

"That was true," Jack had admitted gloomily to himself. After the housemaster had returned to his apartment, he, Rip and Lem resolved to turn over a new leaf.

This was after Mr. Maher's parting shot: "I'm going to have to find a way to stop this nonsense."

These words now ringing in his ears, Jack wondered what J. J. would do. The present returned sharply as he realized that Mr. St. John, the headmaster, was speaking in low, solemn tones, as he did when delivering a lecture. . . . More . . . Jack squirmed in his seat. Could he be imagining that the headmaster was looking directly at him and Lem and Rip? This seemed unlikely, because Mr. St. John was talking about apples.

"I should like to tell you the story of the bad apple," he said. "You all know how close and tightly packed apples are in a barrel. One bad apple can spoil the entire barrel!"

He paused for a moment, and now it was painfully clear that his gaze was indeed fixed on the trio. The whole student body was staring at them.

"Here at Choate," Mr. St. John went on, "we have several of those bad apples—a group of boys who, deliberately and contrary to the good of the student body, have formed a club. They call themselves Muckers! And I believe that these boys, members of this organization, are deliberately trying to change the good order of things at Choate for their own amusement and selfish willfulness.

"Now I am certainly not going to allow such an organization to continue at Choate. I have already written to the parents of these boys. I will speak with them and I will tell them simply that unless this club is disbanded, unless their sons give evidence, strong evidence of a change in ways, they shall be summarily expelled from the school."

Jack's heart sank. In truth, he had not done his best, and he could feel that, sitting there among the student body, Joe's eyes must be downcast in shame for a brother who had brought disgrace to the Kennedys.

"Dismissed," Mr. St. John said.

It was a silent three who returned to their room.

"He said, 'expelled,'" Lem Billings muttered.

"But he sounded as if we might be given another chance," Rip Horton put in hopefully.

Jack was silent. What would his father say? Why had he allowed fun to turn him into a failure? He moved to the window and gazed out on the beautiful Choate campus. The tall, lofty elms cast shadows that looked like accusing fingers pointed at him.

A voice at his rear was saying, "No more Muckers." Rip sounded sad.

"No more," Lem echoed.

Jack turned and silently shook his head.

Their door opened and Joe came in. Jack waited for him to scold. Instead, he gazed at the three and when he spoke, sounded kind.

"I'm sure you've learned your lesson," he said. "So don't just stand there brooding. Buckle down. Out with the books; we all make mistakes."

Then he vanished.

"Joe can do everything," Jack said.

"You're smart, too," Lem put in loyally. "Look how you remember things. You know almost all the answers on 'Information Please.'"

"Yep," Rip Horton said. "What a memory!"

"Oh, great," Jack said. "Say—do you know where I put my khaki pants?"

The Muckers did disband, and, during the following years at Choate, Jack wove an uneven pattern of progress. His English instructor, Mr. Tinker, though appalled at his pupil's penmanship, predicted a future for young Kennedy in putting prose together. Jack's interest in current topics grew, and his reading of *The New York Times* kept him up to date on world affairs.

He already realized that the great Depression, which wiped out many fortunes here in America, had created deep unrest. Perhaps he even sensed that the Russian Revolution had reflected a change of thinking among the poor in every country. Veterans of the war were selling apples on street corners, the laborer was demanding a larger share for his daily toil, and more child labor laws were going into effect.

As for his own family, Jack must have known that his father's fortune had not been affected by the market crash. Though money was not discussed in their family, he was old enough now to understand that possessions were purchased. Two more beautiful homes now belonged to his family—one in Hyannis Port, Massachusetts, the other in Palm Beach, Florida. In both places, during their holidays, the children would swim, sail and become as fearless and competitive on the sea as they were on land.

Meanwhile, though, in spite of resolve, Jack did not settle down to a routine of discipline that would make his father proud. This was reflected in a letter written to his father during his senior year at Choate. Jack wrote:

> Lem and I have been talking about our poor work and we have definitely decided to stop fooling around. I really do realize how important it is that I get a good job done this year, if I want to go to England. I really feel, now that I think it over, that I have been bluffing myself about how much real work I have been doing.

His father was now in Washington and working for his old friend, Franklin Delano Roosevelt who was no longer Assistant Secretary of the Navy but President of the United States. Joseph Kennedy seemed pleased with his son's spirit. His answer, in part, read:

> Now Jack, I don't want to give the impression that I'm a nagger, for goodness knows I think that is the worst thing any parent can be. . . . After long experience in sizing up people I definitely know you have the goods and you can go a long way. Now aren't you foolish not to get all there is out of what God has given you? . . . I am not expecting too much and I will not be disappointed if you don't

turn out to be a real genius, but I think you can be a really worthwhile citizen with good judgement and good understanding.

Whether it was because his good friend Lem had chosen Princeton as the college of his choice or whether Jack decided it might be better for him to be removed from a scene where Joe's glory put him in the shade, it would be difficult to say. At any rate, he decided not to go to Harvard.

"Will your father mind?" Lem asked.

Jack told his friend he wasn't sure. He added that he imagined his father was pleased he had gotten good enough grades to get into a top-flight college.

"Great," Lem said. "Come to Princeton and be my roommate."

Jack decided to go.

"The three 'bad apples' together again," he said.

They threw back their heads and roared with laughter.

4

✿✿✿✿✿✿

AT HYANNIS PORT

RULES WERE RULES here at Hyannis Port, and even guests had to keep them. Jack gazed toward his sleeping friend. In spite of already having been nudged three times, Rip was still out like a light. Curled up and relaxed, he looked as innocent as a babe. It was too bad this had to be remedied, but rules were rules.

At Choate the Chinese torture treatment usually worked when one of the trio tried to drown out the gong by ducking under a pillow. Jack went to the bathroom, wet a washcloth with cold water and returned to release evenly spaced drops on Rip's forehead.

He stirred and mumbled, "Cut it out, Jack."

More drops.

Rip moaned. His eyelids briefly fluttered, but closed again.

Enough of this! Jack spread the cold washcloth over his friend's face.

47

Rip shot up like a jackknife, looked around and said, "What's the big idea? No classes up here—let me go back to sleep."

"Sleep? You know it's seven-thirty."

"So . . . ?"

"So it's time to get up or Joe and his friend Tom Schriber will have licked the larder clean."

"Who's hungry?"

"I am, you lazy landlubber. Come 'join the Navy and see the world!' "

Jack jerked the covers off his friend.

"Lem Billings told me," Rip said, "but I didn't believe him. I didn't believe it when he said he had to take a rest cure after his vacation here. Well—what must be, must be."

Fully awake now, Rip gazed at his grinning friend and added, "Do you know what you look like before you've brushed your hair? An anemic cave man."

Then he caught hold of Jack's bushy forelock, clung, and soon the two of them were at grips in wrestlers' holds. The tussle ended with Jack's shoulders pinned to the floor. Rip Horton was one of the best men on the mat at Choate, and he gazed gloatingly down on his victim.

"Say 'uncle,' " he commanded.

"I will, my eye," Jack replied. With a quick and unexpected maneuver, he released himself from Rip's restraining hands and dashed into the bathroom.

There he appraised his face in the mirror. As always, stocktaking was not merely an evaluation, but rather a comparison of himself with Joe, with whom he could never catch up. Joe was taller and stronger; his features had fine regularity while Jack's own, from the standpoint of conventional good looks, were sadly wanting.

If Jack had been able to admit his best points, he would have seen a pair of large, expressive eyes and well-shaped lips of width and fullness, which throughout his life would remain boyishly curved even when he was angry. Instead, he saw a nose too short, a chin too long, and that hair—! Enough for two heads, and bristly. He grimaced as he brushed, while slicking back his auburn mane with lotion.

Soon he and Rip were padding down the stairs in sneakers, drawn to the dining room by sudden hunger pangs and the sound of voices. Evidently there had been a plan to treat the late-comers as culprits, because, when they first came in, nobody spoke.

"Morning, everybody," Jack said airily. "For those who don't know, this is my friend, Rip Horton."

Silence was briefly maintained, but the irrepressible Kick broke in and said accusingly, "You overslept. Hi, Rip."

"Hi."

Joe looked up from his bacon and eggs, and said, "Good morning, lads. I see you're in training for Princeton."

"What do you mean by that crack?" Jack asked.

Joe smiled and said, "Oh, I hear you're not eligible there unless you can sleep till noon." He must have noticed, then, that Horton looked annoyed, because he added hurriedly, "Just our way of joking, Rip."

"Of course," Rip said. "Harvard humor."

Jack knew his brother wasn't really kidding. Neither

he nor his father had quite got over the fact that he
had chosen to go to Princeton instead of Harvard. Indeed, his father had expressed disappointment about
his decision, but did not press the point.

Their mother came in then. After greeting Rip, she
surveyed the children's plates to see that they had
eaten all that was set before them, then rang for the
maid to bring in more breakfast.

"Milk, too," she said. "Everybody drinks milk at the
Kennedys'. There's nothing better for the health." This
was stated with such finality that no guest would dare
refuse.

All during breakfast, plans for the day were discussed. No form of activity seemed to go unmentioned:
calisthenics, sailing, swimming, tennis, touch football.
Even young Bobby used lingo like a coach.

"What kind of calisthenics?" Rip asked weakly.

"All kinds," Eunice explained. "We have our own
instructors for every kind of sports. Do you like sports,
Rip?"

"Yes, quite," he said politely. "But I doubt that I'll
be able to keep up with this family."

"Rubbish," Jack put in loyally. "Rip was one of the
best wrestlers at Choate."

"That he was," Joe agreed. "And, if I remember cor-
rectly, you play a pretty professional game of golf too,
Rip."

Rip murmured modestly, "Not quite that," but
praise from Joe was enough to give anyone status in
the eyes of his sisters.

"Be on my side when we play touch football, will
you, Rip?" Eunice asked.

"No, mine," Pat squealed.

"No, mine," Kick insisted.

Wanting to please all, Rip smiled uncertainly, but their mother put in, "You can choose sides later, girls. Maybe Rip would like to have a game of golf with your father this afternoon."

Surprised, Jack asked, "Is Dad here?"

"Yes," his mother said, "he decided to take the week-end off, and drove up from Washington last night."

Jack noticed the slightly startled expression on Horton's face. The only time Rip had met Joseph Kennedy was when his father had come up to Choate to square things away with Mr. St. John about The Muckers. No doubt his friend was remembering the tongue-lashing tirade heaped upon their heads, for Jack's father had been furious.

Not wanting Rip to think that the episode would be remembered, Jack said, "Dad doesn't hold grudges. When he's sore, he speaks his piece, but then it's over, Rip."

"Great," Rip said. "I'm anxious to meet him again."

After much food and several rounds of milk, they all poured out onto the porch. On one side was a huge table with a battery of phones, and, close by, a ticker tape machine. Beyond the big house a long stretch of beach lay white in the early sun. In contrast, the grass on the large, well-tended Kennedy lawn took on a darker hue. Beyond the beach a breakwater jutted out, securing yachts and craft of residents who spent their summer vacations in that beautiful spot at Cape Cod.

Jack breathed in deeply the salty tang from the sea.

As his eyes roamed far beyond the Sound, it didn't seem to matter that his previously plastered-down forelock now rippled in the breeze.

"I love this place," he said, almost to himself. He gazed around him before coming to a decision that might end in a minor battle with his brother.

"I want to take *Victura* out today," he said finally.

"Sure, Skipper," Joe agreed. "So the Princeton Tigers want to bare their teeth. We'll come along, won't we, Tom?"

"Sure," Tom Schriber said.

"But we won't do a lick of work," warned brother Joe. "The Tigers will be taking over."

"Suits us," Jack told him.

Just then, two figures were sighted far down on the beach, sprinting along the wet sand.

"Here comes Dad," Eunice exclaimed. "I bet he wins the race."

Actually, their father was not running to win, but had taken the athletic trainer along to set a pace. Joe, Sr. was lithe, fit and lean, and at a distance it was difficult to distinguish between the two men, though his companion was many years younger.

"Beat you to him," Kick shouted, and the girls were off, as serious and intent as if they were competing in the Olympics. Only Rosemary remained behind, watching with the air of one too shy to engage in such tomboy antics.

Bobby took off after the girls, but when he saw that the race had turned into a sprint to his father and back, he whirled around to be first at the starting point. Eunice came next, followed closely by Kick, whose flushed face and smoldering eyes showed fury at having been beaten.

"You didn't play fair," she accused her younger sister. "You decided the rules and started back without telling us what you were going to do."

"Don't be a spoilsport," Eunice said.

"Anyhow, I won," Bobby put in.

The two men moved up then, Joe, Sr. urging Jean along by soft pats on her rear, and scolding because she had not run back all the way. To her protests that the others were bigger, he said, "Don't alibi. Nobody expected you to keep up with the others, but you didn't have to stop."

He turned to his young son and added, "And you, Bobby—don't pretend you won when you only went half the way."

He then turned his attention to the guests, greeting Rip with the warm cordiality of a perfect host.

"Good to see you again, Horton," he said, with not the least sign of remembering the Mucker episode. "Maybe we can have a round of golf while you're here, if the wires don't get too hot." He pointed to the battery of phones on the porch, where he would soon be engaged in keeping track of the activities of big business.

"It would be an honor to play with you, sir," Rip said in his best prep-school manner.

Once aboard the *Victura*, Joe and Tom ducked into the cabin as they had said they would. On deck, Jack and Rip took charge. Soon the sail was hoisted, and, as it was bellied by the breeze, Jack piloted the small craft out into the Sound.

He was glad his brother remained below so that he and Rip could handle the craft together. They occasionally engaged in slangy nautical talk, but for the most part the friends simply soaked in the sun and tasted salt on their lips. Then suddenly the sun lost its warmth, and the taste of salt was supplied by spray beating against their faces. Overhead, what had been an innocent-looking cloud swelled into angry arrogance.

"Squall coming up," Jack said. "I hope you can swim, Rip."

"Passably," Rip told him. "But, brother! where's the shore?"

Rain came slanting down in sheets, and the *Victura* bobbed and dipped. A voice from below came muffled against the whistle of wind.

"Hey, Tigers, do you need any help up there?"

Joe's tones were vaguely teasing, but Jack knew he would come on deck if he was asked.

"No, you landlubbers," he shouted back.

With Rip's help he brought his craft around. By the time Hyannis Port was sighted on the horizon, the squall and rain were over.

Ashore again, Joe slapped him on the back and said, "You handled that one well."

Somehow, this was like being offered a bar of chocolate a long time ago when his bicycle fell and he bumped his head. He wasn't going to take it.

"You knew that squall was coming up," Jack said accusingly.

Joe smiled.

"Sure," he admitted. "Any good skipper consults the barometer before he sets out to sea."

It was humiliating in front of Rip. Joe wasn't going to get around it with a bribe.

"I'm sorry you kids are soaked," his brother went on. "Go up and get a rubdown before we go in swimming."

"Stop giving me orders, Joe," Jack said. "You can't be the big cheese around here all the time. Anyhow, Dad's home."

Joe's voice was warmly sincere when he said, "I am sorry, Jack, but you can't do things half-cocked. Sooner or later you've got to buckle down and plan before you act."

Jack didn't answer. They moved to the porch, where Joe, Sr. was busily engaged in phone conversations, with a receiver to each ear. Besides listening to two conversations, he was dictating to a secretary at his side.

The girls and Bobby came streaming out the front door, dressed in swimsuits.

"We've been waiting for you. You're late," Kick said. She noticed the boys' dripping clothes and exclaimed, "You look like two drowned rats."

"Keep quiet, Kick," Joe told her. "We got caught in a squall, and Jack and Horton here brought the ship in like real pros. Princeton would be proud of them."

Rip smiled. "Jack did it all," he said. "I was just ballast."

"That's not so," Jack put in loyally. "Rip was a perfect mate."

The two of them went upstairs, took brisk rubdowns and put on their swimsuits. Back at the pool Joe was waiting, and suggested he and his brother have a race. Jack knew this was another way of saying again that he was sorry, because Joe rarely beat him.

"Race, race," Kick cried. "I'm rooting for Jack."

Kick usually rooted for the one she thought would win.

Their swimming instructor came up.

"On your mark, set, go!" he said. Jack and Joe dove in, their scissors strokes churning white the water. At first, Joe forged slightly ahead, but when they touched the far end, Jack turned and moved with quick decisiveness. Neck and neck, faster, pulling hard . . . You can't catch me with a paddle, Mr. Maher. . . . You can't catch me this time, Joe.

They sat on the edge of the pool.

"Never saw you swim better, Jack," Joe said, throwing an arm around his brother.

"Thanks."

Joe was a great guy. He was right about doing things half-cocked.

The two J's smiled at one another.

There were twelve at the table for dinner, ten Kennedys and their two guests. The youngest Kennedy, three-year-old Edward—whom everyone called Teddy —had already eaten and was upstairs in bed.

After they were seated, Eunice looked around and asked, "How come no 'big-shot' company this evening?"

Her mother looked pained and said, "I can't imagine

why the nuns permit you to use such slangy expressions, Eunice. In my day, one could tell a convent-bred girl by her language and diction."

Eunice nodded and said, "I know—but things are different now. In those days all a lady was supposed to do was 'sit on a cushion and sew a fine seam.' Now we're allowed to think."

Her mother sighed and said, "You make it sound as if excelling in needlework created a barrier against using yours brains. It seems just the opposite to me. Maybe a little more attention to feminine things might be good for all my girls."

"No use trying," Kick put in. "I'm sure the nuns think we're all hopeless—except Rosemary. She's the only lady in the lot."

Rosemary smiled and looked shyly at her plate.

"Quite true," Rose Kennedy said. "But it's nothing to boast about, Kathleen."

Her husband, though, seemed to find this exchange very funny. He espoused women's right to be part of the world scene and compete with men—to a reasonable degree, of course—because, heaven knew he admired nothing more than an attractive, well-dressed woman like his dear Rose, whose figure was as youthful as any sixteen-year-old's.

He patted his wife's hand and told her not to worry about the girls. In time, he felt sure, they would have the rough edges rubbed off, but meanwhile they were a bunch of healthy, wholesome youngsters.

Rose Kennedy agreed that this was so, but reminded him that Eunice was almost a young lady now, and added:

"If I didn't watch her, she'd go to dancing school in sneakers."

Eunice tossed this off, saying, "The kind of boys I like are more interested in what I say than in my feet."

Their father laughed again and replied to her original question about why no "big shots" had come for dinner. Sometimes he got fed up with their big brains and two-bit bickering. He went on to say how near-sighted these businessmen could be, for instance in their attitude toward the President. FDR had saved the American system of free enterprise and pulled the country out of its slump, he said, but the Republicans didn't know better than to bite the hand that fed them.

"You should see how some of them kowtow to me now," he added bitterly. "After the way they squealed when Roosevelt made me chairman of the Securities and Exchange Commission."

This was true. Many people, even loyal New Deal Democrats, had been aghast when Roosevelt named Joseph Kennedy to control the unstable activities on Wall Street. Here was a multimillionaire tycoon, they reasoned, who had engaged in speculations and played the market with such skill that his was one of the few fortunes which had not suffered during the Depression.

"Yes," Joe, Sr. went on thoughtfully, "Roosevelt saved this country from revolution. So let the economic royalists call him names. Socialist, nonsense! He's no more Socialist than I am—and, though I've been called many names, that's not one of them."

He continued along these lines, with everyone joining in about the Civilian Conservation Corps and other

New Deal measures. Even the girls chimed in, especially Eunice.

She addressed herself to the young men guests, explaining, "Sure, we believe in free enterprise around here. You can tell that. But wasn't it silly for people to be screaming about individual initiative when there wasn't work for people to do, until the President made work?"

There was discussion about that. Then, Joe, Sr. again took up the original theme—that he was happy to get away from the bigwigs for the weekend.

"Besides," he added, "there are things I want to talk about with Joe and Jack."

He sounded quite serious, and Jack wondered whether his father was going to bring up the subject of college again and express his disappointment because he had not chosen Harvard. He doubted that his dad would, however, in front of Rip. Though his father was frank and outspoken before the family, he rarely criticized his children when guests were present.

After dessert, Tom and Rip evidently imagined that their host might want to have a private conference with his sons. The two guests suggested a game of touch football with the girls.

"Just as you like," Joe, Sr. said. "But I thought maybe we'd have some man-to-man talk in the study."

In spite of cries of protest from Kick and Pat, Tom and Rip admitted a preference for the "man talk."

"Good," said Joe, Sr. He rang for his secretary and told her that if any calls from Washington came through, she should say he was in conference and didn't want to be disturbed.

Now they were in the downstairs den, where coffee had been served, a special concession and reminder that men could be permitted more than milk. All in all, Joe, Sr.'s attitude was on a level that suggested equality, and invited a meeting of the minds. Thus, he turned to Tom Schriber and asked:

"Were you surprised when I sent Joe abroad to study with Harold Laski, Tom?"

The young man hemmed and hawed a little, obviously fearful of making a critical judgment to one his senior.

"Don't hold back," Joe, Sr. commanded. "If I hadn't wanted your opinion, I wouldn't have asked."

Tom admitted that he had wondered why a man in Mr. Kennedy's position had sent his son to study with a Socialist.

"Of course," he added, "since he has come back and we've discussed the matter, I realize he wasn't affected by Laski's views."

Joe, Jr. laughed and said, "That's where you're wrong, Tom. I was affected all right, but not in the way the master hoped. He explained my preference for capitalism as 'a mind unawakened to realities.' We did have some terrific arguments, though, and Laski pointed out that here in America we were moving closer to his views. Said someday we'd have a welfare state with many more government controls."

"Do you think we will?" his father asked.

"Not in his sense," Joe said. "Social reforms, yes. But I don't want too many of them, either. It weakens people if you help them too much."

"What do you think about all this, Jack?" their father asked.

"I'm not sure," he said. "I never am until I examine both sides. Take the difference between the Republicans and Democrats, for instance. The Republicans think that if business is good the worker will get his share. The Democrats think if employment is high, business will be good. Of course, you can't work if there is no work around, but if wages get too high there'll be no profits for the owners."

Here he gave a wide grin, and added, "The trouble with me is, when I start thinking, I see points on every side."

"That's not a bad trait, Jack," his father said. "But you haven't actually been exposed to many points of view. That's why I'm sending you over to study with Laski this summer."

"Oh, no!" Jack moaned. "I'm sure I'll feel the same way about Socialism as Joe. Besides, I can get all the economics I need at Princeton."

"How can you be sure?" his father challenged.

Jack knew he couldn't be, but he didn't want to go to the London School of Economics. He wanted to stay here and swim and sail, have his friends up, and laze in the sun.

"It's not so bad, Jack," his brother put in. "Though I must say my social life was pretty dim. I made up a little poem:

> I do here and now insist
> That I never, never kissed
> A female economist.

"Oh, great!" Jack said.

"I'm not sending you abroad to study girls," his father said.

"Oh, do I have to go, Dad?"

"Yes," his father said. "I've already enrolled you there."

In London, Jack found himself challenged by new concepts, and he mingled with people from every walk of life. He enjoyed dressing casually, and unless one had been told, no one would ever have suspected that he was the son of a multimillionaire. Laski's classes drew young people from all over the world—radicals, revolutionaries, and others like himself who were there to sharpen their wits by mental dueling with a mastermind.

Unfortunately in the middle of the summer, Jack was stricken with a case of jaundice and had to return to Hyannis Port.

One day while his brother was convalescing, Joe, Jr. asked:

"How did you feel about the lady economists, Jack?"

"Not too bad," he replied.

But they were not like the girls he would be dating at Princeton!

5

✿✿✿✿✿✿

VISIT TO THE WHITE HOUSE

JACK WAS PAMPERED and petted much that summer, sometimes, it seemed to him, too much. One symptom of his particular type of illness was a constant feeling of fatigue. Family concern and being cared for added to a sense of guilt about being too weak even to want to win.

He almost wished that tenderness would turn to teasing, and Joe would bait him so he'd be forced to fight; but Joe did not. He played the Big, Big Brother to the hilt, and treated Jack with much the same tolerant attitude as he did little Bobby. This was understandable, of course: Joe was strong; he never got sick.

Only the irrepressible Kick maintained the same attitude of mischief, to make him feel that he was neither on the brink of the grave, nor decrepit.

One day when she had brought him a mid-meal snack, she said, "Slant up your eyes, Jack."

He did so, with his thumbs.

Cocking her head on one side, she viewed him seriously and remarked with her usual candor:

"You look like Admiral Togo, the Yellow Peril."

Their mother, who had come up quietly, scolded:

"What a thing to say, Kathy! It's unkind to be personal about things people can't help. Besides, you shouldn't suggest ill will of other people and call them names. Admiral Togo used to visit our home often when your Grandfather Fitz was Mayor, and I remember him as a perfect gentleman. Where did you ever get that 'Yellow Peril' notion?"

"From an article I read in a magazine," Kick said. "It told how someday the Japanese will be our enemies, but it was just sort of fiction."

"I should say so," her mother replied. "Our countries are on the best of terms."

At that point this was true, but subtle forces were already at work, which would bring that day of infamy when Pearl Harbor was attacked.

"Anyhow," their mother went on, "Jack's jaundice is disappearing. You shouldn't have mentioned it."

Jack stood up for his sister.

"Why not?" he asked. "Everybody's being so solicitous and polite, I almost wish they'd take a poke at me."

This must have been relayed to the rest of the family, because the old competitive spirit was resumed and Joe started to razz again.

By August, Jack was on his feet again, receiving his friends and planning their future at Princeton. He had another visitor one day—the genial, smiling Honey

Fitz, who had just returned from South America, where he had been sent by the President as an ambassador of goodwill.

Grandfather Fitz had always scorned calling him "Jack," since this grandson had been named John after him. As always, he kept up a stream of amusing conversation, joking about how the London air had made John sick. What Irishman could stand too much of that English fog, he questioned, to say nothing about their high and mighty airs?

"Yes, Johnny," he went on, "the more I see of other countries, the better I like my own."

His recent jaunt to South America made Honey Fitz sound as if he were a veteran world traveler.

"When you talk about 'our country,'" Jack teased, "what you really mean is Boston."

"And sure, that's where I was born and bred," Honey Fitz said. "Besides, I don't have to visit every State in the Union to know Massachusetts surpasses them all."

He went on, then, to tell about his experiences in South America and about the gay *señoritas* who couldn't hold a candle to his Rose.

"Slim as a reed, she is, your mother, with all her children. But the *señoritas* spread."

He outlined a circle with his arms, to denote the female Latin figure, and added, "And the young ones, bold as brass, were batting their big eyes at me, like I was some young rapscallion."

Jack roared with laughter.

"I'm sure you can hold your own with the best of them, Grandpa Fitz," he said.

"Evidently, you can, too, my lad," was the reply.

"It's the honey-tongue of the Fitzgeralds you've inherited. And I want you to use it, when we take our trip."

"Trip? Where are we going?"

Making it sound quite casual, his grandfather said, "Oh, just a small excursion to Washington, to see the President."

Unbelieving, Jack asked, "What President?"

"What other is more worth seeing than the President of the United States?"

Honey Fitz explained that he had an appointment with his friend FDR, who wanted to hear about South America.

"So get out of those khaki pants and sneakers, lad, and make yourself fit for the White House."

Jack's awe at the idea of meeting the President was quickly dispelled. After they were announced and ushered into the large chamber, Franklin Delano Roosevelt greeted his grandfather with the familiarity of an old friend.

"I brought my grandson along," Honey Fitz said. "My namesake, John Fitzgerald Kennedy—Joe's boy."

Jack felt his hand encircled by a warm, firm clasp, and saw the President's strong-featured face relax into a smile.

"So you're Joe Kennedy's son," he said. "He often mentioned you."

Flashing his own wide grin, Jack said genially, "I imagine it was my brother Joe that Dad mentioned. He's the real brains around our house."

"Now don't sell yourself short, Johnny," Honey Fitz put in. "We all have our special talents."

The President agreed. "And from the reports I've heard about your trip to South America," he told Honey Fitz, "you created quite a stir by singing 'Sweet Adeline.'" FDR threw back his leonine head and roared with laughter.

"That I did," Grandfather Fitz boasted. "And in Spanish, too!"

"Yes, so they tell me," the President said. "'*La Dulce Adelina*'—the Spanish version sounds much more romantic than the Anglo-Saxon, but I wouldn't advise you to try it on the barbershop quartet!"

They joked for a while longer, then his grandfather spoke of more serious aspects of his journey. He told how down there, good will for the neighbors in the North was colored by their own deep problems.

"I've never seen such poverty," Honey Fitz went on. "Conditions among the peasants are worse than serfdom in the Middle Ages. Children starving while the ruling classes roll in wealth." He paused, then used one of FDR's labels for those who were unwilling to share part of their wealth. "Talk about your 'economic royalists'!"

The President listened as if he were unaware of these conditions, but he was not.

"The leaders had better wake up," he said. "What happened in Russia could happen in the rest of the world, changing misery for something worse. We don't want Communism in our hemisphere."

From his reading of *The New York Times* Jack knew that his own father believed FDR had saved the American system of free enterprise by his social reforms. He also knew that most people with large fortunes considered the President's methods dangerous, a trend toward "Socialism" through government controls. He suddenly realized FDR was speaking directly to him.

"How do you feel about these matters?" he asked.

"I haven't decided, sir," Jack said. "To form an opinion, I always have to study both sides, and as yet I don't know enough to have made up my mind."

"A very commendable attitude," said FDR. "But final judgments are sometimes altered by the heart." He smiled then—a sad smile—and added, "Of course, my enemies would deny that I have a heart and claim that my reforms are merely to gain personal power. This isn't true. Most people, when they speak of 'freedom,' are thinking only about themselves. The rich will have to take into account freedoms of the poor. Freedom from fear . . . freedom from poverty . . ."

Now, FDR was alone with his thoughts. Little could Jack suspect that someday he would be seated in that highest seat, where, in spite of advisers, pressures, loyalties, and criticisms, to be President is a pit of loneliness.

Perhaps Jack's decision to go to Princeton had been a symbol of his first effort to break away from handed-down opinions and judge himself apart from the shadow of a "better brother." At any rate, the decision was his own, and when he joined his friends at college, it was with new resolve to mend his ways.

First and foremost, he would have liked to excel in athletics, which would make no demands on his coming to terms with opinions he was not yet ready to form. This he was denied.

Because of his recent illness, his participation in sports was forbidden, except for a moderate amount of swimming. To make up for this lack, he became Rip's manager, espousing his friend's new venture into the boxing ring as enthusiastically as if it had been his own. This was a time when Jack had to find pleasure in the accomplishments of others, which he did with genial good humor.

Because of his illness, he was unable to enter Princeton until several weeks after classes had started. Instead of moving into a fine suite of rooms his father could well have afforded, he chose to live with his friends, Rip and Lem, in old South Reunion, a dormitory that had seen better days. There he was greeted by his friends, who led him to their quarters with the mock ceremony of ushering in a king.

"Does the throne room suit Your Majesty?" Lem Billings teased.

Jack gazed about at the dark relics of furniture, unpainted walls, and curtains sagging sadly on their rods.

He played right along, saying, "It suits me fine, but it's far too lavish for my jesters."

After that, the three had a rollicking, raucous, old-time Mucker scrap, which ended by a reminder from Rip:

"Remember, gentlemen, we're at Princeton now."

In spite of encouragement from his energetic manager, freshman Rip did not become champion of the year.

"You're not going to throw in the sponge, though, are you, Rip?" Jack asked, after his friend had unsuccessfully battled Bill Moore, a clever boxer who had had more experience in the ring.

"No, definitely not," Rip told him.

Then there was the day when the Harvard football team came down to play the Tigers. As long as Jack could remember, the acme of achievement had been held to be the winning of a letter for his father's alma mater. And here Jack was, sitting on the other side! When he saw his brother Joe seated on the Harvard bench, he needed the baiting of his friends to bolster him against a twinge of family loyalty.

"Are you sure you know who you're rooting for, Jack?" Lem Billings asked.

"Of course."

"Then declare yourself, loud and clear," Rip challenged.

But for all his rooting for Princeton, he couldn't help becoming angry when the Harvard coach did not call his brother from the bench. No matter what childish spats they had had or more recent rivalries, the image of Joe was fixed as a hero in his mind. Why was that Harvard coach so stupid as to keep Kennedy out of the game?

Harvard was "slaughtered" by a score of 35-0. On his way to look for his family after the rout, Jack heard that his brother had been kept out of the game because of a leg injury. When he found them, his father's face was more woebegone than Joe's.

"It couldn't have happened in my time," he said glumly.

Ignoring this, Joe put in, "I've got to hand it to you. The Tigers really roared."

Not to be overheard, Jack said softly, "They wouldn't have roared so loud if you'd been in the game, Joe."

The three smiled, Kennedys together.

More and more Jack would have followed the path he had chosen and would have made a niche for himself at Princeton. But again he was drawn back by an unexpected circumstance to what his father had really wanted. A few weeks after the fateful game, Jack was again stricken with jaundice. The doctor decided he had gone back to school too soon, and insisted that his patient take the next semester off to relax and build up his strength. By the time he had recovered, Rip and Lem were a class ahead of him. Since being with his friends had played a large part in his decision to go to Princeton, it didn't seem important that he should be there anymore.

Still, when he told his father, "I think I'll go to Harvard," it seemed that Fate had again stepped in.

During his first few years in Joe, Sr.'s and Joe, Jr.'s alma mater, Jack's drive to succeed seemed centered mainly on athletics. He tried out for as many teams as possible—football, swimming, golf—and though he didn't manage to establish himself as tops in any sports, his severest critics could not have denied him E for effort.

In his freshman year he gained the respect of his future roommate, "Torby" Macdonald, who was later to be an All-American halfback on the Harvard team. Tales of Jack's dogged determination deal with his staying endlessly after practice to toss passes to his friend Torby, for whom grit on the gridiron was a cherished quality.

"We might as well quit—it's too dark to see the ball, Jack."

"Just a few more, Torby; I've got owl eyes."

"Danged if I don't think you have," Macdonald said, and added affectionately, "Don't you ever get enough?"

Jack didn't. He joined the Junior Varsity, from which he was subsequently dropped because of lack of weight, but not before he had received a spine injury that was to affect his entire life.

Indeed, he seemed willing to jeopardize his health in other ways, if by doing so he could possibly enhance the athletic record established by two other Kennedys. Torby, now his roommate, had learned that trying to discourage Jack from taking risks merely resulted in a jutting chin, flashing eyes, and the old "streak of stubbornness."

Jack and Joe, Jr. were having dinner together.

"I hear you're trying out for the swimming squad," Joe said.

Jack said that he was.

"I've also been informed you have a mighty sweet backstroke," his brother added.

"Not bad," Jack told him. "But that chap Tregaskis is also trying out for the team. He's better all around than I."

As a rule, Joe would have given him a pep talk. This time, though, he took a different position. After

casting his eye toward Jack with unusual concern, he
said:

"Have you checked on your physical condition
lately?"

"Why do you ask—am I yellow?"

"No, you're not jaundiced, but you certainly don't
look fit. Is everything O.K.?"

Almost too quickly, Jack answered, "Sure, everything's O.K."

Actually, he had been feeling miserable, feverish
and heavy-headed. He wasn't going to admit this,
though, because Joe might try to discourage him from
trying out for the swimming team. So, since the Kennedy rule rejected coddling, Joe let it go at that and
spoke of other things. He told about some smart aleck
who had made a snide remark about Honey Fitz.

"One of those would-be blue bloods," he went on
angrily, "so *nouveau riche* and fresh from the steerage,
he has to put on a British accent and brag. When I
catch him, his mater and pater will wish they'd waited
to send Junior to an orthodonist, after I take a crack at
his teeth."

When Jack didn't answer, he added, much annoyed,
"Don't you think that's what he deserves?"

"Sure, I suppose so," Jack answered reasonably.
"But I'm not sure it might not be better to ignore that
kind of chap. That would really put him down."

"What kind of fighting spirit is that?" Joe demanded.

"Not very good, I guess," his brother admitted. "But
it's not because I wouldn't be sore about anybody criti-
cizing Grandfather Fitz. I suppose I'm wrong, but to
me silence seems more effective."

He knew that if Joe had gone on, it would have been to say, "I just don't get you, Jack," but instead his brother let the subject drop, and put in, "You'd better check in with the doctor. I've got to go now. Ted Reardon and I are taking out some girls."

And Jack thought that perhaps his brother's suggestion might be wise. He really did feel miserable. Probably he had a little cold; he would get a couple of pills to nip it in the bud.

The doctor's brows seemed to be beetling as he gazed steadily into Jack's face.

"If you don't keep your mouth shut, how can I get a reading?" he asked.

Jack, who had been trying to let cold air in on the thermometer, clamped his lips tight.

"Well, now, let us see," the doctor said as he drew the glass stick out. He shook his head and added, "Hum-m-m . . . Headaches, coughing?"

"No, nothing to speak of," Jack told him airily.

The man took out his stethoscope, put the tube against Jack's chest, and listened. Finally, he said, "You've got a touch of flu; it's almost epidemic around here. You'll have to go to the infirmary."

"For how long?" Jack asked.

"I should say for about a week."

"A week!"

"That's what I said, Kennedy."

Brother! How was he going to compete against Tregaskis if he was to be laid up that long? Jack returned to his room and told Torby the bad news.

"You've got to help me, Torb," he pleaded.

"How can I?"

Jack spelled his plan out. He could never keep up his strength with the bland fare served in the infirmary. So it was to be Torby's duty to sneak in steaks and malteds whenever he could manage. He managed quite often, but meanwhile Jack had enlarged the general scheme.

"You've got to let me know when no one's in the pool, so I can go practice," he said.

Torby balked.

"You'll really be sick," he protested, "and where will that get you?"

But Jack was so insistent, so absolutely adamant, that if his friend would not be part of the conspiracy, he would sneak to the pool himself—and probably get caught and also sacked.

"What can I do?" asked Torby.

Torby did keep a lookout for his friend, who, despite fever and weakness, managed to improve his stroke. But even after taking this dangerous chance Jack did not make the team. Still no one could have said he hadn't tried.

About this time there was a marked upheaval in the Kennedy clan, when FDR appointed Joe, Sr. Ambassador to Great Britain. To say this event created a stir on all sides was to put it mildly.

Many Boston blue bloods were aghast that the President had so little tact as to name an Irishman and a Catholic to serve at the Court of St. James's. But then, they bitterly asked one another, could one expect a Roosevelt, a renegade to his class, to do differently?

No less humor and derision popped into old-time

political Hibernian heads. Imagine the son-in-law of
Honey Fitz and the son of that good son of Erin, old
Pat Kennedy, kneeling in knee britches before the
Queen of the blasted British Isles!

Talk or scoff who might, there was never a time in
Joe, Sr.'s life, when he had so much cause to be proud.
This was a post previously held by men of great stature
—even two former American presidents, John Quincy
Adams and James Monroe.

It is interesting to speculate whether FDR might not,
at least subconsciously, have given the somewhat belligerent, outspoken Joseph Kennedy the appointment
to annoy those "economic royalists" who had never
ceased sniping at the President. If so, Roosevelt's
jest backfired, because it was over the issue of help to
England that the two finally fell out. Joe, Sr.'s dealings
with the British suggested the conflicts of a man who
had never been able to rid himself of resentment toward a country that had oppressed his ancestors.

At the time of his father's appointment as Ambassador, Jack seemed quite aloof from world affairs and
from the frenzied activities of fellow students who were
taking sides on New Deal reforms, unrest abroad, and
"ideologies."

No doubt the feverish left-wing groups considered
the son of a multimillionaire a lost cause in any liberal
movement. With the right-wingers he was also suspect,
because his father served under FDR. So if Jack had
chosen a label he would have been a middle-of-the-
roader, but he hated labels and wasn't ready to choose.

He did, however, take part in the more traditional
campus activities, such as working on the *Harvard*

Crimson, the well-known student newspaper. His duties there were in the business end of making the newspaper a success, rather than on the editorial side. Thus he could avoid expressing opinions not yet formed. Then again, as a member of the Hasty Pudding Club, he need be taxed no further than to decide what musical comedy should be put on.

Meanwhile his seven younger sisters and brothers had been taken out of American schools and placed in schools abroad. Rosemary and Eunice sailed together to join their mother at the embassy in London, where she was engaged in many and varied duties as wife of the Ambassador to Britain.

At long last, in his junior year Jack was touched by the turmoil preceding war. As a student of government and politics, he became eager to see firsthand those forces abroad which bore directly on his studies. With this in mind, he persuaded the Harvard authorities to let him spend the second half of his junior year abroad. In March of 1939, as the Nazi troops were invading Czechoslovakia, he sailed across the sea to become a spectator to terrible history in the making.

6

✫✫✫✫✫✫

THE AMBASSADOR'S AIDE

THE WORLD had *not* been made "safe for Democracy," by World War I. The League of Nations, on which Woodrow Wilson had based his dream for world peace, had fallen apart. The Versailles Treaty had become a scrap of paper to be torn up and thrown to the wind. Power-crazed leaders disregarded all law, and two dictators had met to divide the world between them.

Both the pompous Mussolini, founder and leader of Italy's Fascist movement, and Adolf Hitler, Germany's Nazi Fuehrer, made their appeal to people according to the trend of the times. Hitler promised the Germans, stung by defeat in World War I and burdened with economic problems, that he would restore the rights of the common man. He pandered to national pride by building up in the Germans' minds the idea that they were superior to any other people. Mussolini, an ex-Socialist who in reality wanted to restore the Roman Empire in order to keep himself in power, also played on the heartstrings of the poor.

While at first both dictators claimed to be champions of the underdog, they later used the overthrow of Marxist Bolshevism as an excuse for setting out to conquer. In their own countries they destroyed all democratic processes by ruthlessly murdering or imprisoning anyone who might oppose them, and they cared nothing for human life or the dignity of man.

Earlier, in 1935, Mussolini's troops had invaded Ethiopia, and in spite of Haile Selassie's pleas at the League of Nations, the free world was not ready to intervene. In 1938 France and England had signed with the German Nazi dictators the Munich Pact, which was intended to "bring peace in our time." But it had delayed Hitler's entrance into Czechoslovakia for only a year.

Although the Axis armies were not yet ready to engage in world conquest, Hitler's storm troopers were already entrenched in Austria. There Socialists as well as Catholics, Jews, and peasants had been slaughtered or imprisoned by the Gestapo.

Next on the Axis timetable were Poland, the Scandinavian countries, Belgium, Holland, France and —as a plume in the tyrants' caps before conquering America—the British Isles. But so far these moves had not been made.

This was the general situation when Jack arrived at the embassy in London. There he was to survey only briefly the social life of his family. He heard about his mother's success as a gracious hostess to Europe's most important people and of his sisters' helpfulness in arranging diplomatic gatherings, of how Eunice was admired for her efficiency and brains, and how Kick, his own special pet, was being courted by a high-ranking peer.

A Frenchman who knew the Ambassador's daughters catalogued their charms in this way: "Eunice is the most intellectual and Pat's the prettiest, but Kathleen is the one you remember."

For Jack, however, there was not much time for entertainment and frivolity. Joe, Sr. had more serious business for his sons. In his post as Ambassador to Britain, their father had to relay to Washington all facts, rumors and detailed information about the turmoil in Europe. Jack and Joe were added to his large staff of roving reporters, to gather all available data about matters that might affect America's interests. Jack traveled to many countries, mixed with people, and listened to divergent views.

Although details about information Jack forwarded to his father are fragmentary, some of his personal observations are known—and many of his conclusions proved accurate. For instance, from Poland he wrote: "Probably the strongest impression I have gotten is that rightly or wrongly the Poles *will fight* over the question of Danzig."

In Russia, Jack got his first glimpse of the sprawling, giant country freed by revolution from Czarist tyrannies some twenty years before. Although many of the early Communists had fought for the rights of the workingman, at the time of Jack's visit there was little freedom for anyone, for the country was under the control of the dictator Josef Stalin, who had "eliminated" his enemies with the same despotic ruthlessness as his Fascist and Nazi counterparts.

Although Jack merely wrote, "This is a crude, backward, helplessly bureaucratic country," the plight of the downtrodden people and the bleak windswept streets of Moscow and Leningrad could not have failed to make a lasting impression on his mind.

As his father's confidential aide, Jack also visited the Crimean Peninsula and from there took a ship to Istanbul. Thence to Jerusalem, where he wrote to his father about the touchy British-Arab-Jewish situation and described himself as being totally in accord with British policy.

Later his stay abroad took on a lighter aspect. Torby Macdonald had come to Europe with the Harvard track team, but took time off to join his roommate on some of Jack's continental jaunts. A brief interlude was spent at the Kennedy summer home on the Riviera, but the blue of the Mediterranean, dancing, small talk and fun were not the primary order of the season this particular year.

Now the world was waiting to see whether Hitler would carry out his threat to invade Poland. Jack and Torby were sent to Germany to get a firsthand impression of reactions there. During this visit, Jack, Torby, and another All-American halfback, Byron White, were attacked with a barrage of stones thrown by Nazi hoodlums.

Torby and White were all for giving the bullies a

sound thrashing, but Jack, as son of an American ambassador, felt that open conflict might cause embarrassment to his father. Nonetheless, he reported the incident and added that this episode was but one reflection of an outpouring of hate directed by Germany against the British.

A small seam, which would later divide his views from those of his father, was starting to show. Free of Joe, Sr.'s deep-rooted Irish-English hostility, Jack was beginning to admire the British.

On the other hand, his father had and would retain a single-minded purposefulness against involving America in any situation that might threaten her neutrality. At that time most of his countrymen would have concurred. World War I was sorely remembered; why should our boys again fight on foreign soil? However, most Americans also deplored the destruction of democratic Czechoslovakia, and the majority abhorred the ruthless methods used by the Axis powers against minority groups and other innocent people.

On a second visit to Berlin, where he stayed at the American embassy, Jack found the atmosphere charged with sinister threat. The large embassy mansion, once a happy meeting ground for American citizens, was shrouded in darkness. All light bulbs had been removed and the phones disconnected. In lowered voice, Alexander Kirk, the U.S. chargé d'affaires, told the reason for this curious blackout.

"John," he said, "war is very near. The date has been already set. Go to your father and tell him that the Nazis will strike within three days of the anniversary of the battle of Tannenburg, which was August 27."

Since the embassy officials wanted their awareness of these plans to remain secret, Mr. Kirk urged Jack to leave at once and to make sure his mission was not detected.

On September 1, 1939, the Nazis declared war and marched into Poland, with which country both Russia and Germany had a nonaggression pact. When it became apparent to Stalin that the Germans were ready to march, he rushed his own troops to occupy the eastern section of Poland. Dictator Stalin and the Fuehrer themselves had signed a mutual nonaggression pact, a vivid example of the axiom that there is no honor among thieves. Hitler, who was "going to save the world from the Bolsheviks," had suddenly become their buddy!

Twenty-four hours after the outbreak of hostilities, Jack became personally involved in a situation bearing directly on the war. The Kennedys were staying at the Ambassador's summer home, a country house near London, which still seemed out of danger. It was three in the morning and, as the family slept, an emergency call came through for Joe, Sr. He was informed that the British ocean liner *Athenia* had been torpedoed in the Atlantic. He was also told that the survivors would probably be landed at Glasgow, and that three hundred of the passengers on the ill-fated ship were American citizens.

Jack's feeling about being awakened at such an hour was reminiscent of Rip's reactions when he had

tried to rouse him at Hyannis Port. This, however, was
no game calling for "the Chinese torture treatment."
His father's voice was urgent.

"Get up, Jack. I'm sending you to Glasgow."

Was this some sort of joke? Not even a streak of
dawn in the sky.

"Glasgow?" he asked sleepily.

"Yes. Up with you, now. A British ship was torpedoed with three hundred American passengers
aboard."

Jack was up in a flash, and full of questions.

"Does this mean we'll go to war with Germany. . . ?
The *Lusitania* was one of the things that got us into
the last war."

"I can't say," Jack's father told him. "Much will
depend upon the circumstances. If the ship was carrying arms, the Germans could claim that this was provo-
cation. These are matters I want you to find out. Be
of whatever help you can to our nationals. Keep me
informed."

If his father was troubled then, he would have
been more so had he been confronted by the victims
of the Nazi submarine. There was no neutrality among
the passengers, who without warning and in cold
deliberation had been fired upon.

To establish facts accurately, Jack interviewed
members of the crew. He learned that the ship carried
no armaments. He spoke to as many survivors as possible while doctors and nurses hurried about, tending
the injured. Even those fortunate enough to have
escaped injury presented a pathetic scene. Women
were there with children in arms, covered only by

blankets they had managed to rip from their beds. There had been no panic; all had behaved bravely, but anger was the keynote of their mood.

Fearful that they might be torpedoed again on another passenger ship, the survivors loudly demanded an American convoy to escort them home.

Jack tried to reason with them. America was still neutral, he explained, and the presence of United States battleships might provoke a war.

To this, one angry passenger answered, "We've got six billion dollars worth of United States Navy, and they won't do this for us!"

Jack wired and phoned all the facts to his father, who in turn cabled Washington. It was arranged that a liner of the Ward Steamship Company would go to Glasgow to pick up the survivors and take them home.

"We don't want a passenger ship—the only thing the Nazis will respect is a warship—we want a convoy!" was the declaration of those who had spent weary hours battling the sea.

Jack comforted them to the best of his ability and tried to give assurances that the Nazis would not dare fire on an American ship. "They wouldn't chance dragging us into this war," he said.

But wouldn't they? This act of ruthless aggression made it seem that Hitler was quite willing to take chances. Such were the questions seething in Jack's mind when he returned to Harvard for his senior year.

Jack's firsthand contact with the situation abroad had made him "quite a seer around here," he wrote his father. Evidently he had become a figure of interest outside the campus. John Alden, a reporter for the *Boston Globe*, interviewed the Ambassador's son soon after his return to the United States. Alden wrote:

> Handsome, tall, thin, and high-strung, with an ingrained habit of cocking his leg over the arms of his chair, young Kennedy is having a hard time, after such an exciting seven months, in settling down to the humdrum life of a student. Radios, chairs, laundry and valises were scattered helter-skelter in the three-room suite at Winthrop House.

The reporter was correct in assuming that Jack was suffering from the problems of settling down. A new dimension had been added which made his previous attitude toward his studies seem immature. His firsthand observations had given him a realistic interest in international politics. He registered for extra courses to make up for his lost time.

Professor Holcombe, who had flunked Jack's father in Finance and was willing to make wry digs about that former student's success in the field, now had praise for the son. Concerning Jack, he later observed:

> Kennedy came back from working in his father's office in London a greatly matured man. His mental powers were much greater, sharper. He was a keen observer. He would not commit himself to a position until he was sure. Then he would always give himself leeway to compromise or modify his position.

Along with his mental awakening, Jack also took a more active part in the social life of Winthrop House.

Nonetheless, his roommate Torby and a chap named Ben Smith were sometimes at a loss to explain the change in the Jack they knew. Both these men were first-string athletes, and although Jack could be called upon to appreciate their prowess in the field, his chief interest was improving his scholastic grades. This he did, and pulled his mediocre average of C up to A's and B's. He was then eligible to graduate with honors, which required the writing of a thesis.

Jack chose for his thesis the subject, "Appeasement at Munich." He set down his own observations, which were strengthened and analyzed in frequent consultation with his professors. This thesis was in many ways stiff and pedantic in style, but objectivity placed the work on an intellectual level. He dug deep for reasons behind the Munich Pact, and believed that to blame the few figureheads who had signed this treaty was superficial and shortsighted. He wrote:

> The critics of Chamberlain have been firing at the wrong target. . . . The Munich Pact itself should not be the object of criticism but rather the underlying factors, such as the state of British opinion and the condition of Britain's armaments which made "surrender" inevitable.

Jack pointed out that democratic nations such as Great Britain and the United States might not be able to stand the test of war without sacrificing democratic traditions. He pointed to Britain's unpreparedness, which he felt was a warning for America to rearm as fast as possible. His country must not be strangled by apathy nor deceived by wishful thinking.

Meanwhile the Nazi machine, equipped with tanks and bombers, advanced like a malign steamroller leveling damp cement. Holland and Belgium first, then the vast French network of the Maginot Line, collapsed like a cardboard house.

Only England fought on—and her army was flung back to the sea at Dunkirk. Thousands of boats—every type of craft—sailed to rescue the British soldiers from complete annihilation.

Thus when Jack Kennedy graduated from Harvard, with all the pomp and pageantry of an Ivy League commencement, the whole of a continent was in flames. Jack was graduated *cum laude* and received a *magna cum laude* for his thesis. Jack's mother and sisters came from England for the exercises, but his father could not attend. Joe, Sr.'s absence was softened by a cable containing a message which must have warmed Jack's heart!

TWO THINGS I ALWAYS KNEW ABOUT YOU—ONE THAT YOU ARE SMART. TWO THAT YOU ARE A SWELL GUY. LOVE DAD.

Jack's thesis was so well received by his professors that he decided to send it to Wilfred Funk, Inc. The work was accepted for publication and its title changed to the more provocative one: *Why England Slept.*

The book sold forty thousand copies in America and an equal number in England. Thus at twenty-three Jack had become an internationally known author.

7

✫✫✫✫✫✫

A WORLD AT WAR

WHEN THE WAR got under way, Joe, Sr. sent the rest
of his family back to America while he stayed on at
the embassy. It seemed certain to him now that the
British Isles would soon become the first-line battle-
front. He was a man who had always played to win,
and although he had at times taken chances, he considered the Allies' plight a totally lost cause.

In June 1940, Nazi troops had pressed on into
France, and the road to Paris lay open before them.
To stay in favor with the Fuehrer, Italy had declared
war on France and Great Britain. Just before the
French government fled to Bordeaux, Premier Reynaud broadcast a final appeal to President Roosevelt
for American help, rather than give the word to his
armies for a cease-fire. Reynaud resigned and the
aged Marshal Pétain became the figurehead who would
deal with the Nazis.

"It is with a heavy heart," he said as he announced the armistice to his country, "that I tell you today that we must stop the fight."

Hitler was already counting on victory over England in the belief that his bombs and blockbusters would quickly bring the British to their knees. He did not know that Churchill's stirring words, "We shall fight on the beaches, we shall fight on the landing grounds, we shall fight in the fields and in the streets," expressed the spirit of most of his countrymen.

Joseph Kennedy did know, however, that after this stirring speech, Churchill had turned to the Dean of Canterbury, who was sitting beside him, and said, "And we will hit them over the head with beer bottles, which is all we really have got."

In truth, the British actually were preparing to fight off Hitler's invasion with beer bottles containing sulphur and TNT. To Joseph Kennedy, the Allies did not have a "Chinaman's chance." Furthermore, he was seeing firsthand the terrible consequences of war—bombed-out British towns, people maimed and killed. This he did not want to happen in his own country. He did not realize that the cards were already stacked—America was on the blueprint, a juicy peach waiting to be plucked and divided among the victors on the Axis side.

Meanwhile, the Russian Bear had started to prowl, and while nibbling away at Finland, sent out the news that her little neighbor was responsible for the Reds' aggression! This was the beginning of the Communists' grand grab of the countries around them.

In Hyannis Port, however, the Kennedy family was far enough removed from the war that they, like most other people, still held to the hope that America would not become involved. Still their grand reunion that year could not completely turn their thoughts from what was happening. For the first time in America's history during a period of peace, the selective service system had been put into effect. Why would young men be drafted into the armed forces, unless the country expected to go to war?

There at Hyannis Port, sunlight streaked gold the riffled waters of the Sound. It was good to be alive! Maybe terrible things wouldn't happen tomorrow. College friends of both J's came to visit and engaged in constant rounds of swimming, boating, golf, touch football and tennis.

Still, activity could not quite wipe away awareness that all was not the same. Young Joe, after a year at Harvard Law School, had already made a niche for himself in the political arena; Kathleen was a newspaperwoman on *The Washington Times-Herald*. Jack, as the successful author of *Why England Slept*, had attained stature in the family and confidence in himself. Now, it was quite naturally assumed that Joe would be a politician and Jack a journalist.

Friends poured into Hyannis Port for weekends and at once were recruited into some kind of team. A certain amount of tact was required because, although the rivals were out to win, one dared not criticize the other side too severely, since it also contained loyal Kennedy fans!

When sports were over and family and friends sat down at the table, talk had a way of turning from books and theater and sports to the "trouble abroad." Here at home, most political discussion dealt with the coming election, and whether it would be wise and proper for Roosevelt to run for a third term.

Since it was fairly well known that Joe Kennedy, Sr. was against all military aid to Britain, and the President had already made ships available to bolster her far-spread fleet, many people wondered why Roosevelt allowed the Ambassador to remain at his post. There was also much speculation about whether Joe Kennedy would back the President for a third term. Joe Kennedy, Sr. would, but Joe, Jr. would not. This time the son had taken a stand before he had learned of his father's decision.

Meanwhile, the two brothers debated and argued their differences throughout the summer. Now it was evening, and a crescent moon lay low on the horizon. The sun still vied with dusk, bathing the scene in a rosy light. Weekend guests had gone, somewhat frayed by the constant round of frenzied activity, but feeling more physically fit than when they had come.

Eight-year-old Teddy had beguiled Jean and Bobby into taking a hike along the shore, with the promise that he would bring back the largest and best collection of shells ever scooped up by human hand. For those who remained behind, there was an unusual urge to reminisce, to dig into the past and so forget the future.

Pat stirred in her chair and said, "It would be a beautiful night for a sail. Do you remember the time you and Tom Schriber stayed in the cabin during a squall, Joe?"

"I sure do," Joe said. "Funny how long ago that seems."

Eunice, "the most intelligent," put in her views about the sense of time. "It's because so many things are happening now—so many unpleasant things," she said. "The present is so full of problems, it makes the feeling of being completely free for fun seem far away."

"I suppose that's the reason," Jack said. "One can't stop thinking about the war and wondering what's right."

"Do you mean about getting in?" Joe asked.

"Yes."

"But this isn't our war, Jack," his brother said. "Believe me, I'm not heartless, but what were the British doing while Germany rearmed?"

"You know I agree it was shortsighted and stupid for other countries not to have rearmed, too," Jack said. "Also shows bad Intelligence. But this was partly because people thought Hitler was mad—they didn't take him seriously. This was blind, but look how the British are holding out—what they did at Dunkirk. Besides, I don't believe the spirit of France is dead. Some leader will come along to rally them, bring them back to their ideals of freedom."

"And what will they fight with?" Joe argued. "Armaments we send them—and get us into the war? You're being very romantic, Jack."

His brother was silent for a moment, then said, "I don't think so, Joe. Hitler told of his intentions in

Mein Kampf. 'The world tomorrow,' he said. At the rate he's going, he'll carry out his threat if something isn't done."

"Marxist philosophy says the same thing," Joe reminded his brother. "Their aim to 'divide and conquer' is worldwide, too."

"That's so," Jack conceded. "But the Russians aren't ready to go it alone. Look at the fight little Finland put up against them. Hitler's letting his so-called ally nibble at Poland, Latvia and Estonia, but just let the Russian armies so much as blink toward the Balkans, and the Fuehrer will start shouting about a holy war again. He might even forget what happened to Napoleon and try to invade Russia."

"Would you want to come to the rescue of the Commies, Jack?" his brother asked.

"That's not the point. This is the second time Germany has set out to conquer the world, and I don't want goose-stepping storm troopers cluttering up our beach. No, I'm not being romantic, Joe."

Dusk had become victor over the sun and now the crescent moon reigned over the heavens. Figures had become slatelike silhouettes, but the tones of voices betrayed separate identities.

"Speaking of romance," Eunice put in, obviously trying to take a lighter vein, "I have a hunch all the Kennedy girls will end up spinsters. We have so much fun in our family, who would want to exchange it for a man?"

"Speak for yourself," Patricia piped up. "I'm going to find me a Prince Charming—a movie star."

"You would," Eunice said, then added mischievously, "All brawn and no brains, I guess."

"Oh, no," Pat told her sister. "Both brawn and brains."

After a pause, Joe said reminiscently, "Say, Jack, do you remember when we were little, Dad asked if we thought he should sign up Red Grange for one of his movie productions?"

Jack told him he remembered this very well, and they both went on about how they had urged Joe, Sr. to give Red Grange the part, which had proven wise because the football hero's picture had been a tremendous hit.

Laughing, Jack said, "Our first business venture."

They continued to draw out tidbits from bags of memory, recalling The Muckers and their mischievous exploits, which caused Joe to say:

"You sure didn't show much promise at Choate, Jack."

"That's what you thought," Jack disagreed. "You were so busy being boss, you didn't realize I was sharpening my imagination to become an author."

" 'Imagination!' " Joe exclaimed. "A very low level of imagination, I'd say. You Muckers ate your way through Choate."

"That we did," Jack admitted. "Ah! Those waffles Mrs. Maher used to make—and what a miserable time The Muckers gave her husband."

Soon, however, the conversation came around to the present and FDR. Joe expressed his opposition to a third term.

"George Washington set the precedent against it," he said, "and no one could say those weren't troubled times."

Jack considered this before replying, then said thoughtfully, "True, but if the Founding Fathers had thought the issue important they would have written it into the Constitution."

"Maybe," Joe said, "but FDR is not going to be my candidate. Dad thinks the world is big enough for both democracies and dictatorships, but the way Roosevelt's behaving we'll be dragged into the war. So, as a delegate to the Democratic National Convention, I'm not going to switch from Farley."

Eunice said, "I wonder what Dad will do."

All were astonished when Kathleen's voice sounded, torn with mixed emotions.

"I don't want us to get into the war either," she said. "But we sit here and talk, talk, talk, while England's being battered to bits. It's all very well to be impersonal, but I can't help thinking about—" Here she paused, too overwhelmed for words, but after a brief strained silence, she went on, "If things keep on this way, I'm going to quit my job at the paper and go back to England."

Seeing that her heart was heavy because of one across the sea involved in battle, the others tactfully refrained from further talk on the subject. Fortunately, Bobby, Jean and Teddy returned just then, Bobby demanding that they play charades. Came a click and the porch was flooded with light, and activities were resumed.

In October the Ambassador came back to the States to speak on Roosevelt's behalf in his bid for a third term. He had been given a warm send-off by the British, including a key presented by Their Majesties and the two Princesses. To show his appreciation of the honors received, Joe, Sr. expressed in his best diplomatic manner his respect and affection for the country in which he had served. Of the terrible bombings, he said: "I did not know London could take it. I did not think any city could take it. I am bowed in reverence."

The President, knowing how his old friend felt about lend-lease to Britain, summoned Joe, Sr. before he had a chance to express his views to reporters. Roosevelt must have convinced the Ambassador that he did not intend to "take this country into war." Aid to England Joe, Sr. now accepted, but he was still adamant about military involvement in the Allied cause. As yet both President and people shared his views. Thus Joe, Sr.'s radio speech backing Roosevelt for a third term was described as "probably the most effective vote-getting speech of the 1940 campaign."

The Ambassador, however, went further at an informal meeting with a group of reporters, which he claimed was "off the cuff."

He said, "I'm willing to spend all I've got to keep us out of this war. . . . There's no sense in our getting in. We'd only be holding the bag. What would we get out of it? Democracy is finished in England. It isn't that she's fighting for Democracy. That's the bunk. She's fighting for self-preservation, just as we will if it comes to us. As long as she can hold out, give her what it takes, whatever we don't have to have, and don't expect anything back."

Obviously, Joe, Sr. was not then "bowed in reverence." Furthermore, he was politically naive in supposing that his "off the cuff" comments would remain a secret. His remarks were reported and created a storm in Britain, especially the reference to democracy's being finished there. At home an editorial in *The New York Herald Tribune* said, "If Mr. Kennedy is not an out-and-out advocate of appeasement, he is nevertheless a defeatist of the first water."

Joe, Sr. countered his critics by saying that he thought the interview wouldn't be reported, that the published story "creates a different impression entirely than I would want to set forth."

Nonetheless, he sent in his resignation as Ambassador to Great Britain, and it was promptly accepted. He had alienated his friend FDR, who, as in the Fore River incident long ago, had got his own way.

However, even if Joe, Sr. might have been prejudiced against the British, he was all the same a deeply patriotic man. His was an honest difference of opinion, and when subsequent events suggested his shortsightedness, he was man enough to acknowledge that he had been wrong. When the attack on Pearl Harbor came, he volunteered his services to the President, but they were not accepted.

Meanwhile, he could have tried to influence his two sons against joining the armed forces of their country, but he did not. Nor did he use money or influence to try to get his boys a soft berth. As when Joe, Jr. had stuck with Farley and political cohorts wanted the father to interfere in Roosevelt's behalf, he took the stand that his sons were quite capable of making up their own minds.

Joe, Jr. had modified his views about the war and had come to the conclusion that America was indeed threatened. In June 1941, he enlisted in the Naval Air Force. Twenty-seven other young college men arrived at the Squantum Naval Air Base that June morning along with Joe Kennedy, second class seaman. Word must have got around of his enlistment, because a batch of reporters were lined up to greet him. Some of their queries were sharp edged, showing that Joe, Sr.'s stand was still remembered.

"How does your father feel about your joining up?"

"My father completely approves of what I've done."

"Then the Ambassador must have changed his mind about the general situation. Is it because the Japs are rattling sabers?"

"Why don't you ask him? My father's no longer Ambassador to Britain, but speaks as a patriotic American citizen."

"What are your future plans, Mr. Kennedy?"

"I'm in for the duration. After that, I hope to return to Harvard and get my degree in law."

"What about your brother? Is he still soft on the Munich Pact?"

Joe bridled and almost shouted, "My brother never was. But some of you fellows are so anti-intellectual, you panic when a person starts to think."

He consented then to have some pictures taken, to bolster up morale and influence other recruits to sign up. Then, Joe stated that he was simply one of a group of twenty-seven, and that he thought his companions' reasons for signing up were as important as his own.

Jack, meanwhile, was confronted by problems in joining the armed forces. His first choice would have been the Air Corps, but he knew that the back injury received on the football field at Harvard would disqualify him. Later he tried to join the Army, but was rejected because it was thought the grueling chores of an infantryman would put too much strain on his back.

Vexed at not being able to prove his mettle, he set about, under the direction of physical training instructors, to alter the situation. For five months he went through a series of strenuous exercises and finally won a commission in the Navy. But instead of being assigned to combat duty, he was given an Intelligence job that took him no further than a desk in Washington.

On Sunday morning, December 7, 1941, Japanese aircraft bombed Pearl Harbor, and wiped out a large portion of the American fleet. We were at war!

Fighting for your country at a desk was unendurable. Jack used all his influence and his father's to gain a combat assignment. Although it was with a heavy heart that Joe Kennedy, Sr. agreed to "pull those strings," he did not try to dissuade his son.

Late in 1942 Jack arrived for training duty at the torpedo boat training station at Melville, Rhode Island. There he was regarded as an unusual figure for that kind of outfit. Later a member of the PT boat service recalled his first meeting with Jack at Melville. His name was Paul Fay, Jr., and the scene was thus described:

The first thing I did when I landed at Melville was to dig up a football and round up a bunch of the new guys who came there with me for a game of touch. We started to play and this skinny kid in a Harvard football sweater came walking down the field and watched us. He asked if he could get into the game. I said sure, if he got another guy for the other team, which he did in a few minutes. Well, he wasn't in the game five minutes before he started arguing with me about the rules. I wanted to brain him. I figured he was one of the officers' kids. Well, the next day we started classes on how to operate the boats and it turns out that this same skinny kid is our instructor.

After training, Jack learned that he was to be assigned to a PT squadron which was to patrol the Panama Canal. Again he refused to be shelved in a noncombatant area, and appealed to the Secretary of the Navy, James Forrestal, for duty in the Pacific. His request was granted by this old friend of his father's, and, early in 1943, Jack was shipped from San Francisco to join the attack against Japan then taking shape in the South Pacific. The squadron was based on the island of Rendova, south of New Georgia, where he was made skipper of PT-109, containing a crew of two other officers and ten enlisted men. This was more like it!

8

☆☆☆☆☆☆

LIEUTENANT JACK

IT WAS August 2, 1943. The sky was unbroken by moon or stars as Lieutenant Jack Kennedy piloted PT-109 in Blackett Strait, forty miles from the base at Rendova. This was the thirty-first mission of PT-109, their loyal, sturdy craft, which had inflicted plenty of punishment on Japanese forces entrenched on the island of New Georgia.

The Japs were being harassed from the air by day, and at night their destroyers were pestered by the swift, maneuverable PT boats, which after discharging their loads seemed to disappear into thin air. The result was such that the Japanese fleet was transferring troops from the island beaches to a safer place to the north.

That night Kennedy was at the wheel and another officer, George Ross, a sturdy, athletic Princeton graduate nicknamed "Barney," was on watch.

"All clear till now," Ross said, scanning the inky sky through his binoculars.

"About as clear as mud," Kennedy replied. "But if we can't see them, let's hope they're at the same disadvantage."

The enemy could have heard them, though, so PT-109 was running on one engine and at low speed. Jack knew that the silence could explode at a moment's warning, but so far, he thought with satisfaction, they had kept the destroyers on the run.

All hands were at their battle stations when a shout from the lookout sounded:

"Ship at two o'clock!"

For a brief moment the crew of PT-109 mistook the Japanese destroyer *Amagiri* for a sister PT boat. Realization came too late. Before a shot could be fired, the enemy destroyer had knifed through sullen waters and smashed amidship into PT-109. Although the craft was cut in two, the terrific impact failed even to slow down the speed of the *Amagiri*.

Two of the crew of PT-109 fell where the ship had parted, their lifeless bodies sucked into the churning trail left by the destroyer as she slid away into the darkness. Soon the shadows were parted by licking flames as one segment of the PT boat caught fire. This section trembled, shook, then exploded and sank.

Lieutenant Jack Kennedy felt himself flung into space, then stopped, as he crashed against the cockpit of the other half of PT-109. The impact of the blow against his back caused anguish so acute that he thought, So this is how it feels to be killed. Then his body slid prone onto the deck.

Briefly he lay still, then drew himself up into a crouching position. As the pain receded somewhat, his mind became suddenly clear. He was not alone; huge gasoline lily pads, ignited on the water, revealed the silhouettes of four crew members. Only four— were there no other survivors? Was Ross here, or was he on the half of the boat that went down?

Kennedy shouted, flashed a light, and saw figures in the water near the still floating hulk. Hyannis Port . . . the pool . . . "You can't catch me, Joe . . ."

He was in the water now, swimming toward members of the crew. One man, McMahon, had been badly burned, and Harris, their engineer, had hurt his leg. Voice guiding, arms tugging, the Lieutenant aided these two back toward safety. The span between the survivors and their goal widened as a breeze blew back the hulk of floating wreckage.

"My leg," Harris moaned. "I don't think I can make it, Skipper."

Lieutenant Kennedy appealed to civic pride.

"For a guy from Boston," he said, "you're certainly putting on a great exhibition out here, Harris."

With the Lieutenant's aid, both Harris and Mc-Mahon did make it.

After all had returned to their doubtful sanctuary, heads were counted. Eleven of the thirteen crew members had survived. Soon, they thought, the two sister PT boats which had been trailing them would appear to pick them up. Dawn came, then day, but no rescuers. Having heard the crash and seen the burst of flames, it had been assumed by members of the patrol that PT-109 had gone down with all hands. And now the remaining wreckage was listing badly, settling.

What to do now? Kennedy suggested they all have a reasonable, democratic discussion.

"There's nothing in the book about a situation like this," he said. "Seems to me we're not a military organization any more."

This did not work. Each survivor had his own opinion, and the Lieutenant realized he would have to take command.

"We'll have to move fast," he said. Then, appraising his crew according to their abilities, he ordered all but the injured men into the water.

A dissenting voice said, "The PT's will be coming along."

"Not soon enough," Kennedy barked out sternly.

This prophecy came to pass at once as the floating hulk started to turn turtle.

Their destination was a small island three miles southeast, chosen as least likely to harbor Japanese troops. McMahon, the most disabled from multiple burns, became Lieutenant Kennedy's special charge. He clamped the two long straps on the injured man's life jacket between his teeth and swam. This method, although cleverly conceived, resulted in a constant stream of salt water pouring into the Lieutenant's mouth.

Whenever he stopped to catch his breath or cough, the skipper tried to buoy up his listless burden, asking:

"How are you, Mac?"

"I'm doing fine, Skipper. How are you?"

"Fine, real fit, Mac."

Swim, strain, splutter, strain, on and on. Slow, painful dragging, seconds, minutes, hours—five long hours. Finally a shoreline and trees inched forward.

All in all, Lieutenant Kennedy had been in the water for fifteen hours, and after hauling Mac over jagged coral reefs, the two lay exhausted on the shore of a small atoll. Jack's eyelids closed, but he pushed back sleep long enough to thank God that this mission, through the help of His grace, had been accomplished. Even then sleep was torn by fleeting thoughts. His mother, father, sisters, brothers—Joe. Where was Joe now? Would the family be informed that he himself had been killed in action, because this was how it must seem. Otherwise the PT boats would have returned to look for survivors. The boats—he must find a way to signal them—he—

After a brief rest, Lieutenant Kennedy decided to strike out on his own to a farther island near Ferguson Passage. This was the regular route of PT boats; he might be able to intercept one. His protective gear consisted of a ship's lantern that had been salvaged from the crash, to be used for signaling, his loyal Mae West, and a 38-caliber pistol hung around his neck. As he shoved off from the reef at twilight, a huge fish knifed through the water close by. Torpedo-shaped, this monster barracuda could deal death far more cruel than an explosive missile with the same sleek, elongated form.

He strained hard, and strained, salt stinging wounds

made by the jagged coral reef. Finally he came to Ferguson Passage. There, numb with cold, he treaded water, cradled his lantern and waited. Waited, and waited for a boat. None came.

At the end of his endurance, he decided to return to the atoll, but the current was faster now and he was tired. So tired and cold and numb he could not swim—could not even care what was happening. Still, the light of the lantern was a small link with his men. Meanwhile, let the current carry him along, moving in circles through the night.

Finally the next morning, the tide turned and he came out of his trance at the exact spot on Ferguson Passage where he had been the night before. It had seemed, as he was being borne along by the current, that he somehow might have died. This was not so; he was alive—must make his way back to his men.

Again he started off and reached the atoll, picking his way over the rough coral reef that pierced and bruised his unshod feet. He retched, vomited, and looked at his companions with glazed eyes.

"Ross, you try it tonight," he said, and Lieutenant Kennedy lost consciousness.

Maybe Ross would have better luck than he, Jack thought, as he lay on his back, blinking toward the heavens. The situation was bad. McMahon was very sick; his deep wounds had become infected. All the men were thirsty, as was he. Fresh water no one could have expected to find, but this mangy little island did not even boast a single coconut tree—but better not think of cool, sweet juice. . . . If they had chosen a larger island, the Japs probably would have been there —far worse to have been taken prisoners.

Faith, hope and charity were strongly implanted by his Catholic training. He had not faltered in faith, and had tried to act in charity—but hope was receding, for himself and his men. No, he would not have it thus. Maybe Ross would intercept a boat. That night he much snatch some sleep so as to be able to do what must be done.

When Ross returned in the morning, he reported failure. During his vigil not one ship had been sighted.

"Well," Kennedy said, "there's no sense staying here. Neither Japs nor Americans consider this place important enough even to bomb."

Together they decided to move the crew again to an island more available to the fleet and where they might at least find food—if only coconuts to stave off hunger pangs, and the fruit's milk to keep them from dying of thirst.

With all the men weakened by their ordeal, this venture seemed worse than the previous one, even if they did not have to swim as far. Against the current, the straps in the Lieutenant's teeth seemed to tug him ever backward—but he inched on and on.

This time they took refuge on a larger island with more protective bushes and brush, and a goodly supply of coconuts. The Greek gods could have found no ambrosia so succulent as that meaty white substance, nor nectar so soothing to their parched, cracked tongues. Yet, as they had been without food for so long, this fare made them ill, and would not stay down. Even so, for the first time the crew slept soundly that night.

Next day, however, they were disappointed to find that there was little chance of rescue if they remained where they were. There was no evidence that the Japs had occupied the island, and it did not seem likely that the Americans would come to a place which even the enemy had bypassed. Beyond was the island of Nauru, which suggested the possibility of moving on again. Screened by the brush, a Japanese barge could be seen moving in that direction. Then came the steady drone of airplanes overhead.

"Down. Don't stir!"

But the winged craft overhead proved to be friendly ones.

"P-40's," Ross commented. "New Zealand planes."

One of the squadron broke away and dumped its deadly load on the island of Nauru.

"They evidently think that place is worth strafing," Lieutenant Kennedy said. "You and I are going there, Ross."

"Roger," Ross replied, "but it could be swarming with Nips."

Could be—but nothing was gained by *not* taking chances. "We'll risk it," the Lieutenant said.

One of the crew noticed then that a man named McGuire wore a rosary around his neck.

"Say, give that necklace a working over, will you," he said.

With not a trace of self-consciousness, McGuire

lovingly fingered his beads, and said, "Yes, don't worry. I'll take care of all you fellows."

Though the Lieutenant's lips did not move, in simple faith he echoed a silent "Our Father."

Nauru Island was only a half mile from their present base, but it took the two men more than an hour to swim there. Weakness and strained muscles, combined with the thought that they might fall into enemy hands, retarded their speed, but they moved forward.

Again beach coral dug deep into their feet as they moved crouching across the island. A cracking twig, air stirred by the flutter of a bird's wing, were enlarged in their ears like sharp reports. The enemy could be anywhere. However, they found only the deserted wreck of a Japanese landing barge and evidence that McGuire's prayers had been heard. In the hulk they discovered a cask of fresh water and tins of stony hardtack. Water, food—! The first since PT-109 had sunk. They feasted.

Again by night, they took up their vigil at the water's edge, but did not sight a boat. Still, with their find of the day before, the trip had been worthwhile! So Kennedy decided to embark on another treasure hunt. When light came, he skirted the island cautiously, since this patch of soil set in the blue Pacific could still become a target for the enemy. That nature had not been lavish in decking the island with fertile greens and foliage turned out to be a blessing in disguise. Behind a clump of sparse brush, and or partially shrouded in the wide-spaced shadows cast from palm trees, Kennedy spied a small empty canoe

That night he paddled out into the passage, hoping to be sighted, but again no rescue ship appeared. At any rate, he decided to use the canoe to carry the water keg and some hardtack from the Japanese landing barge back to the waiting men he and Ross had left behind them on the other island.

This he did, but his small craft was to serve him only briefly. On his return trip to Nauru a tropical squall suddenly blew up and left him struggling in the water. As rain streamed down with flattening force, a large war canoe approached. Had the dark-skinned occupants been unfriendly this could have been his doom. But even in his soaked state, the natives could see that the floundering man was white-faced and not one of the Japs who had been routing their people from peaceful pursuits in their island homes.

They hauled in the fair-skinned stranger and paddled him to Nauru. There he and Ross tried to communicate with the natives in pidgin English. This failing, they added gestures and repeated over and over again, "Rendova, Rendova, Rendova—Americans, Americans, Americans."

Finally the Lieutenant found a small shelled coconut and dug in a message with his knife:

ELEVEN ALIVE NATIVE KNOWS POSIT.
AND REEFS NAURU ISLAND KENNEDY

After handing this to one of the natives, he and Ross again took up their chant "Rendova," and gestured toward that island. It seemed—although one could not be sure—that the man's expression signaled understanding. Before the natives left, they led Kennedy and Ross to a two-man canoe covered over by leaves. Then, after a lively conversation among themselves, they took to their own canoe and paddled off.

Slim hope seemed somehow more fatiguing than the desperation that had driven them on. Ross and Kennedy fell to the ground and passed out. All day they lay on the beach exhausted, but by evening the Lieutenant's mind was tickling with plans again.

"We can't count on anything, Ross," he said.

"True."

"Let's take the canoe and go to the passage together," the skipper suggested.

"Anything you say, Shafty," was the prompt reply.

Jack smiled. His nickname "Shafty" had been bestowed because in his companions' minds it suggested the long, lean, gangling figure. The two set off into Ferguson Passage and the whimsical tropics changed its mood. The sea, which had been serene, was suddenly whipped by winds, and their canoe bobbed on the choppy water like a cork. There was no way to steer or guide the craft, which shuddered briefly, then overturned.

"Sorry I got you out here, Barney!" Kennedy shouted.

"This would be a great time to say, I told you so," Ross shouted back.

There was no more talk, for both needed every ounce of breath to struggle against a current headed for the open sea. For two hours they struggled, then managed to force their way out of the suction and toward the island. As he clung to the upturned craft, a huge wave suddenly broke the Lieutenant's clasp, swirled him around and downward. Had he been bashed against the jagged, knifelike spears of the coral reef, it could easily have been the end. Miraculously, though, he was drawn into a gentle eddy.

Ross had been less fortunate. Jack saw his face, blind with pain from cuts received on his downward fling. His arm and shoulder were stained red with blood, and he seemed unable to move forward.

"My feet," he moaned.

"Steady, Barney, here I come."

His friend's feet were so torn that the Lieutenant had to salvage canoe paddles and lay them down so that Ross would be able to move over their smooth surface instead of the rough coral beach.

Completely spent, they fell on the beach and slept.

When he awakened, Jack Kennedy sensed that he and Ross were not alone. Automatically his hand went for his knife, but, as he looked up blinking, he saw that the faces hovering over him were friendly. Four natives, one speaking in English—beautiful to hear.

"I have a letter for you, sir," he said.

Kennedy tore open the envelope and read:

On His Majesty's Service. To the Senior Officer, Nauru Island.

I have just learned of your presence on Nauru Island. I am in command of a New Zealand infantry patrol operating on New Georgia. I strongly advise that you come with these natives to me. Meanwhile, I shall be in radio communication with your authorities at Rendova, and we can finalize plans to collect the balance of your party. Lieutenant Wincote.

"We're saved, Barney; we're saved!"

Although his infected arm was swollen twice its size and he was in agony, Ross managed a grin and said, "Yes, Skipper, we're saved."

In the canoe and covered by fronds, the Lieutenant was paddled to the New Zealand patrol. Later he contacted a PT boat and went aboard. Guided by the natives, this sister ship picked its way back through shoals and channels to rescue the rest of the crew.

At the Rendova base, the arrival of these men, given up for lost, was marked by wild celebration. Word of the role the Lieutenant had played was told and retold. Such courage and tenacity did not go unrewarded. In addition to the Purple Heart, Jack was awarded the Navy and Marine Corps Medal. His citation was signed by Admiral William F. Halsey, and it read in part:

"His courage, endurance and excellent leadership contributed to the saving of several lives and was in keeping with the highest traditions of the United States Naval Service."

To reporters he later said, "I only did my duty. The real heroes are the ones who never got back."

Joe, Sr., who had received word that his second son was missing in action, now received with gratitude a second message. He wired back the heartfelt words:

THANK GOD FOR YOUR DELIVERANCE.

As was customary following such rugged experiences as those undergone by the crew of PT-109, it was suggested that the men be returned to the States for duty. Lieutenant Kennedy refused.

At Rendova, Al Cluster, his squadron commander, faced Jack and asked, "How come? Most of the men would give their eyeteeth to get home."

"Maybe, but I just got here. I'd like to remain on duty, sir."

Kennedy was assigned to a PT which had been transformed into a gunboat. The extra load of men and ammunition made these reconditioned boats extremely vulnerable. Paul Fay, who was with Jack at this time, described the Lieutenant's activities in these words: "Working against Jap barges close to shore with a slow overloaded PT was really perilous and terribly exposed fighting, but Jack kept at it."

His squadron commander, in recalling this service, said: "It got so that the crew didn't like to go out with him because he took so many chances. He even wanted to make a run up the Choiseul River, which was loaded with Japanese guns. Finally, he began to realize that our experiment with the beautiful little gunboats was less than a complete success, and it was only then that we were able to persuade him to go home and get his back looked at.

"I'll never forget the way he insisted on staying on the job when he had a legitimate reason for returning to the States that any of us would have jumped at. This trait for devotion or obligation, or what-have-you, is, in my opinion, as important a facet of Jack as his courage. It wasn't recklessness, but a mature dedication to service not often seen by any of us."

Jack's "mature dedication to service" had only begun. For the present, though, he was being sent back to the States.

What was Joe, Jr. doing now?

9

✫✫✫✫✫✫

ELDEST SON

JACK'S SAFE RETURN to the States after such close calls
with death became a symbol of hope to his family.
His presence somehow seemed to promise Joe's safety,
too. True, Jack had lost an alarming amount of
weight from his bout with malaria and near-starva-
tion on the islands. This could be remedied, however,
by rest and good food.

"More milk, Jack," his mother commanded when
her son was home on weekend privileges from the
hospital.

He was still a patient there, receiving a series of
treatments for his injured back. Progress was slow
and he was never free from pain.

Before, Hyannis Port had been a haven, in a sense
removed from the harsh realities of an alien world.
If sometimes it did seem that rivalries and competition might crack the kernel of their bond, loyalty held
like granite if a Kennedy was threatened from with-

117

out. And now in the shadow of Joe's absence, family closeness was cemented by mature consideration and understanding. The present was no game with stakes a skinned knee or shin or a bump on the head from some sport. In war the opposing sides were out to maim or kill, and although the tide of battle had turned in favor of the Allies, the last shot could be as fatal as the first.

Joe, Jr., as if to make up for doubting that his country should have gone to war, had insisted on remaining in active service beyond the call of duty. After receiving his commission as a Navy pilot, he was sent to England in the fall of 1943. There he was assigned to a squadron of Liberator bombers attached to the British Coastal Command.

All through the winter, and mostly in bad weather, this squadron patrolled the Bay of Biscay, the English Channel and the North Sea, unloading their bombs to cut the lifeline of German submarines. After a specified number of these dangerous flights, he was eligible to return home, but he asked for another tour of duty. This completed—shortly after D-Day—he was again ordered back to the States.

Just as he was leaving, Joe heard of a secret operation calling for the skill of expert and seasoned pilots. Although his luggage had already been placed on a transport bound for New York, he again postponed leaving. His decision to volunteer for a mission with dangers yet untried was in the old tradition of the Kennedy team spirit.

Jack knew that his own return home safely was

considered as a sign that Joe would do the same. Often during weekends with his family, one or another of them would draw the parallel.

"When we heard you were missing in action, we didn't give up hope—" Or, between long lapses of letters from his brother, it would be suggested wishfully, "Joe probably is taking his leave in London and having a high old time with friends."

This last could not have been really believed because, if it were so, Joe surely would have written. Besides, the chief reason for his going to London would have been to see Kathleen, and she was now here in Hyannis Port. She had served in England as an American Red Cross worker and again met William John Robert Cavendish, Marquess of Hartington. Her old romance with "Billy" was resumed, and in spite of objections from both Cavendishes and Kennedys—chiefly for religious reasons—the two had been married. Love had triumphed and now the tomboy Kick, high in British nobility, had come home to Hyannis Port at the urging of her husband who wanted her to be away from the bombing while he was in France fighting with the Coldstream Guards.

Kathleen and Jack played the game of letting their parents think whatever was most comforting to them. They themselves suspected that the plight of Britain was precisely the sort of situation to tempt impulsive Joe to undertake some dangerous mission.

The two were speaking in undertones on the porch on an evening reminiscent of the time they had all sat around together discussing the pros and cons of America's being drawn into the war. Again a soft breeze riffled the Sound, and late sunlight stamped coral and jade-green zebras on the water. Nature's beauty here had not been altered by man's destructiveness, but all else seemed different.

Jack and Kick were discussing what could have caused Joe to change his mind about returning to the States after his second series of flights.

"It must have been something important," Kathleen said.

On this they had agreed before, but had never allowed speculation to become specific. Recently, however, the first V-2 rocket bombings were in the news, and in spite of Allied victories many feared that Britain would not be able to withstand the terrible punishment.

Not stating definitely what he had in mind, Jack said, "Those bases will have to be destroyed."

He need not explain; Kick knew exactly what bases he was talking about.

"I don't suppose the regular Flying Fortress raids could knock them out—" she ventured.

"No. From what I've heard, the launching site is built of blocks and blocks of concrete, and, even if a plane could get close to the heavily fortified area, conventional air armament wouldn't even scratch the surface. The V-2's fly too high and fast to be intercepted. They'll have to be dug out from their source."

"How?"

"I'm not sure; the Command will think of something."

This was precisely what the Command was doing and why Joe, Jr. had not come home.

He had volunteered for a top-secret operation aimed at putting an end to the destruction of Britain. The plan was to send an explosive-laden Navy bomber close to the German launching site and there let loose twenty-two thousand pounds of TNT.

To raise this heavy load from the ground, the plane had to be manned, and Joe Kennedy, Jr. volunteered to pilot the craft. His co-pilot was another American, Lieutenant Wilford J. Wiley of Fort Worth, Texas. After getting this "Flying Bomb" into the air, the two man crew was to set the controls aiming the plane with its deadly cargo at the V-2 launching site, after which the pilots were to parachute out somewhere near the Channel coast. Only volunteers were considered for the mission. What could have been more challenging to a temperament like Joe's?

Though neither Kathleen nor Jack were certain what was causing their brother's delay, both sensed that his absence spelled danger. So when their parents came out on the porch, their low-voiced speculation was quickly transformed into gay chitchat.

"I can't get over how Bobby has grown," Jack said. "Any minute now he'll be dating."

This attempt at diversion did not work. Instead, as did most subjects now, the mention of a son brought up somber thoughts.

"At least we have one boy," their mother said, "too young for the armed services. That is, unless this terrible war goes on for years. Why must there be all this fighting, when love is such a simple thing—?"

Such sentiments from his mother, Jack thought, were not to challenge God's will but came from a deep, inherent gentleness that could not understand or cope with hate or cruelty.

"What do you mean, 'if this war keeps on for years'?" their father said with assumed heartiness. "We've got the Axis on the run, and soon the family will be together again."

"Of course," Kick agreed.

"—And do you know what I'd like," Joe, Sr. went on, "I'd like all of my children to build houses here at Hyannis Port. There's plenty of beach front." He paused, obviously remembering that his daughter Kathleen would one day be committed to houses and halls, abbeys and palaces in rural England, and Lismore Castle in Ireland. Still he held to the proposition, and went on, teasing, "We'll make an All American out of your Billy yet—teach him a man's game, football—none of this soccer stuff."

Kathleen smiled and said, "Sure."

Jack now steered the conversation into other channels by calling attention to a yacht heading for the open sea.

"She's a beauty," he said.

They all agreed. Eunice, Jean and Teddy joined them, and they went indoors for dinner.

This was the last weekend Jack was to be home for a while, because surgery had been recommended to relieve his injured back. It was hoped that an operation might cure the condition, or at least make it possible for him to move about freely. The family was concerned, but old-time pampering was out of place for one who had endured so many hardships.

Only his mother betrayed uneasiness by saying, "You're still so terribly thin, Jack, and I'm sure the hospital food won't fatten you."

Briefly, there swam into his mind the scene of his crew gagging over coconut meat after not having eaten for days. As always, he managed to mask emotion with a wide, flashing smile.

"You can bring me some chocolate whipped cream pies," Jack told his mother.

This reference to a boyhood passion brought up a train of memories, and all chatted about their childhood, with Joe, the absent one, seemingly more real than those present.

Jack was still in the hospital and confined to bed although the doctors believed that his operation had been at least partly successful. In a case such as his it was impossible to say whether the cure would be permanent, since his spinal injury had been extensive. Still, the pain had been eased, and freed from this nagging, his vigorous spirit took hold.

One morning he felt with a sudden start that to be alive this day was especially good. Why? The heading on the newspaper in his hand read: August 2, 1944, the anniversary of the date PT-109 had been sliced in two. And here he was, hearty and on his way to becoming hale—so all was well in the world, at least almost. Joe, what about Joe? Even this doubt he managed to dismiss by reminding himself of his many escapes by the skin of his teeth. In this mood, he could build on the happy possibility that, since none of them actually *knew* what Joe was up to, he might indeed be cavorting around England meeting new people and charming them with his outgoing friendliness.

Just then the door opened to admit his brother Bobby. Although this younger brother had an absurdly youthful look, he was earnest beyond his years, and now his face wore a particularly serious expression.

"Hi," Jack said to the figure hovering in the doorway. "Don't stand there, my lad. Come in."

His brother moved across the room and, drawing a chair close to Jack's bed, he remarked in carefully controlled tones, "You look great, Jack, great."

"That's how I feel," his brother replied. "As they say, 'fit as a fiddle and ready to go'—and I've been thinking a lot about Joe. You see, this is a sort of banner day for me, the anniversary of being a skipper on half a boat. So, I said to myself, if I could squeeze out of that scrape, Joe—"

He paused. Why had Bobby's steady gaze turned from him, and what made his brother's finely chiseled face settle into a stony, sorrowful mask?

"What's wrong, Bobby?"

Robert's only response was a silent shake of his head.

"Killed?"

His brother nodded.

"When?"

"Not sure. Two priests came and told Dad a few

hours ago. Officials must have thought it was the best way to break the news to him."

"Are they sure?"

"The word was *killed* in action, not missing," Bobby said. "The folks are still hoping; we'll probably get details."

When the account of Joe's death was later reconstructed, it was shown that their hope had been without reality. Joe and Lieutenant Wiley had managed to get the heavily loaded bomber into the air and steer it into a cruising position. It was thought that when they set the fuses something went wrong, but no one could ever know for a certainty what happened except that the plane blew up in two quick blasts and, with its crew, disintegrated in midair.

"It's a terrible blow to all of us," Bobby said that day as he told Jack the sad news.

His brother was speechless. With Joe gone, a sense of overwhelming responsibility settled on him. But he should not be thinking of this now—not of himself, but of his family and Joe. Joe, whom sometimes he had thought of as belligerent, whose bossiness he had often resented as a boy. Their father's first son, in whom he placed his highest hopes, and whose place no other could take. Joe dead? No, this could not be— one so vitally alive could not be gone.

"How are the folks?" he asked in muffled tones.

"Mother is holding up; she's always sustained by prayer. Kathleen is taking it very hard, and Dad—he's trying to act as though it hasn't happened, but he won't be able to keep that up." Here, Bobby shook his head and sat silent in self-communion. When Jack did not answer, he added suddenly, "I don't think he'll ever get over this."

Jack agreed and his thoughts turned to Bobby, who had tried to spare him, and whose admiration for Joe had been limitless. In a gesture of compassion, Jack's hand shot out and was enclosed by a warm firm clasp. They were two, but at that moment, one.

"Take care, Jack," Bobby said in low, clipped tones.

"Roger, will do."

Their eyes met in a lingering gaze of trust.

While Jack was still in the hospital, waiting for his medical discharge from active service, he conceived the idea of compiling a book in memory of Joe. This was to contain reminiscences of Joe by members of the family, friends and others who, because of their admiration for his brother, would want to be included.

When Eunice and Ted came for a visit, Jack discussed the plan with his sister.

"It's a great idea, Jack," she said. "Have you thought of a title?"

"How do you feel about: *As We Remember Joe?*"

"It's simple and to the point," his sister said. "I like it."

"So do I," Ted, now twelve, chimed in. "Can I write something about Joe, too?"

"Of course," Jack told him. He and Eunice went on discussing the work while Ted silently listened. They thought the book should be privately published since the sentiments would be too personal to put before the general public.

"I do think, though," Jack said, "we should let it be known what we are doing, even tell a few people who have been key figures in Joe's life. There are many who'd want to contribute."

This prompted Ted to say, "You promised I can be in it, too."

"You can," Jack told him.

"Like what?"

Eunice considered. "Well—like, how wonderful and strong Joe was—and the way he took care of you, and—"

Teddy cut in and said, "Sometimes Joe wasn't calm —like the day he threw me in the ocean. Can I write about that?"

"Sure," Jack told him. "Say how you feel in your own words."

The naturalness of a twelve-year-old regarding his reactions toward a big brother was more revealing than many of the stylized compliments.

Ted wrote:

I recall the day a year before we went to England. It was summer and I asked Joe if I could race with him. He agreed to this so we started down to the pier about five minutes before the race.

We had our sails up just as the gun went for the start. This was the first race I had ever been in. We were going along very nicely until suddenly he told me to pull in the jib. I had know idea what he was talking about. He repeated the command again in a little louder tone, meanwhile we were slowly getting further and further away from the other boats. Joe suddenly leaped up and grabbed the jib. I was a little scared but suddenly he zeized me by the pants and through me into the cold water.

I was scared to death practully. I then heard a splash and I felt his hand grab my shirt and he lifted me into the boat. We continued the race and came in second. On the way home from the pier he told me to be quiet about what happened that afternoon. One falt Joe had was that he got very easily mad in a race as you have witnessed. But he always meant well and was a very good sailor and swimmer.

Some of the other members of the family and close friends who penned tributes to Joe were Grandfather Fitz, Kathleen, George Taylor, the Negro valet in Cambridge who had been one of Joe's closest friends at Harvard, Ted Reardon, Arthur Krock, and many, many more.

Harold Laski, the economist, added his tribute. He wrote:

He was interested in everything. And there was his astonishing capacity for enthusiasms; what he liked, he liked with all his heart. He had a profound interest in politics and he had his heart set on a political career; he often sat in my study and submitted with that smile that was pure magic to relentless teasing about his determination to be nothing less than President of the United States.

Perhaps the most poignant reminder, in the light of Joe's tragedy, was a letter from Ensign James Simpson, the last person who spoke with Joe, Jr., before his fateful flight. Outgoing and gay to the last, the pilot's

joking reference to the possibility of not returning
was probably not made entirely in jest.

Ensign Simpson's letter said:

> I was in the plane testing and double-checking
> three minutes before take-off. I shook hands with
> Joe and said, "So long and good luck, Joe. I only
> wish I were going with you." He answered, "Thanks,
> Jim. Don't forget you're going to make the next one
> with me. Say, by the way, if I don't come back, you
> fellows can have the rest of my eggs." We never
> saw him again.

Jack's own tribute read in part:

> I think that if the Kennedy children amount to
> anything, it will be due more to Joe's behavior and
> constant example than to any other factor. He made
> the task of bringing up a large family immeasurably
> easier for my father and mother, for what they
> taught him he passed on to us, and their teaching
> was not diluted through him, but rather strengthened.

As a short preface, Jack set down from the Book of
Solomon: "Honorable age is not that which standeth
in length of days, nor that is measured by number of
years. Having fulfilled his course in a short time, he
fulfilled the long years."

Soon again to Jack came another solemn reminder
that war still held full sway. Kathleen, his merry, un-
forgettable child companion, now a lovely woman,
came to the hospital to say good-by to him. Stricken,
she told him that her husband had been killed in

action, that the cabled report was taking her home to Britain. He wanted to protest: Stay, Kick, *here* is your *home*. But she also belonged to Billy's family now, and she must comfort them.

"Sure, Kick, of course, you must go."

After she had kissed him and left the room, he was the one needing comfort—but the eldest son of a Kennedy *does not cry.*

10

✿✿✿✿✿✿

PLUNGE INTO POLITICS

AFTER JACK's OPERATION he had much time to reflect.
His period of convalescence would be long, and the
doctors could give no guarantee that he might not
have recurrent trouble from his injured spine. During
the period when he was too weak and ill to move
about, only the past seemed real, and the terrible toll
war had taken on his family.

Peace, however, was in sight, a wave of hope skirting the ravaged shores. It seemed unendurable to Jack
to be inactive, especially now when the role of taking
Joe's place was thrust upon him. As first son, he must
be strong. So, when the family came to visit, he put on
a front—the flashing smile, the shrug, and sometimes
even an air of cool indifference.

Not that anyone was urging him to make up his
mind about the future—no, not even his father, who
was now sorrowfully living in the past. His visits to
the hospital were brief, and his only direct suggestion
was:

"If you should ever decide to go into politics, Jack, the family will help you in every way."

Neither a demand nor an order, this was said in the vague tone of a broken man. His father's unaccustomed lack of spirit made Jack wish he were ready to carry out what he knew to be Joe, Jr.'s desire. But he wasn't ready; maybe later when he was stronger. He needed more time to make important decisions.

Still, after the unhappy man had gone, the second son who was now the first, could not rid himself of the sense of letting the family down, of failing to do his duty by not at once agreeing to his father's words. Still, he reasoned, one could accomplish little in any career for which he was not fitted. He remembered how Joe, Jr. had enjoyed the game of politics, how he could charm the toughest, crudest ward leaders by speaking their language, slapping backs and engaging in long bull sessions as they smoked big black cigars. He lacked such outgoing qualities—how could he compete?

It didn't seem shameful before, Jack thought, that I found it difficult to crack through reserve and communicate with people unless I knew them well. Why, now, does this make me feel insecure? Sensibly, then, he had analyzed his own special talents. Was it so dreadful, really, that he didn't enjoy coming face to face with personal conflicts but rather found fulfilment in the written words?

He was a successful author, so why not again engage in putting down thoughts now seething in his mind—especially about peace. The war was almost over, and the future must be met. From his bed, Jack wrote an article called "Let's Try an Experiment in Peace." In this he argued for the total disarmament of Germany and Japan and a pact between Britain, America and Russia.

Was not all of humanity looking for a blueprint to prevent future wars? To keep the peace would occupy mens' minds for the unforeseeable future. The bombing of Hiroshima, which would hasten the war's end, was also to usher in the awesome atomic age. Men were faced with the terrible knowledge that this world and all its beauty could be destroyed by an impersonal finger on a button. The world was to become a bristling camp, with the free countries—those permitted to choose their own representatives and uphold the rights of the individual—on one hand, and the Communists on the other. When the war ended the Russians would disregard all treaties and use their advance positions to claim small countries as their own.

Although Lieutenant Kennedy could not then see the exact turn history would take, it was in the shadow of his family's grief over the death of Joe and Kathleen's husband that he was first seriously preoccupied with problems of world peace. At this time, however, this interest did not serve to clarify his own future. As a wan, pain-ridden hero, he appeared before the Navy Board and was retired from active duty.

Home again with the family, Jack realized that no one was going to try to force him into a decision. No matter what his father hoped, he meant to abide by the old rule of letting his children make up their own minds.

"No need for you to jump into anything, Jack," he told his son. "Experiment for a while and find out what interests you."

Jack took himself to task. There must have been that moment when he really stopped trying to be Joe and completely erased from memory their boyhood rivalries—accepted the idea that even if his father would never quite get over the death of his eldest son, this did not diminish the stature of the second. Indeed, if Jack had not come to believe in himself he could never have risen to the stature that he did.

What Jack needed was time, not to *take Joe's place,* but to re-establish a life of his own. It seemed he might find fulfillment in journalism, . . . soon he had his chance, when he was hired as a reporter by the Hearst-owned International News Service.

He was first assigned to San Francisco where the great nations of the world were convening to discuss ways and means to maintain lasting peace. He was assisting at the birth of the United Nations. Aroused now, Jack's lively curiosity took hold as he analyzed and sorted his impressions. First and foremost in his mind was the conviction that the success of this world body would be insured only if the Big Three powers —America, Great Britain and France—continued to remain solidly together. His capacity to absorb, plus a photographic memory, linked all of Jack's experiences into a timeless chain. What he was viewing as a raw reporter—the attitudes of statesmen, moves and countermoves to control the balance of power—would later be remembered when, as President of the United

States, the fate of a world rested on his decisions. Actually he found that diplomatic moves were much like any game, and, although the stakes were higher than those on a Harvard football field, strategy played an important part.

It is interesting to review some of Reporter Kennedy's dispatches:

> For the first seven days in San Francisco there has been so much jockeying for position. . . . The stormy sessions of the first week have done much to clear the air. They have shown clearly the tremendous difference between the viewpoints of Russia on the one hand and the United States and Britain on the other. . . . It is unfortunate that unity for war against a common aggressor is far easier to obtain than unity for peace. . . . There is here, however, one ray of shining, bright light. That is the realization, felt by all delegates, that humanity cannot afford another war.

Later Jack briefly toured Europe for INS, covering the Potsdam Conference between President Truman, Premier Stalin, and Prime Minister Churchill, and tracking down leads on obscure communiques being sent to the States. Curiously, however, this life, which had lured him as a possibility for his future, grew stale and palled. When asked by friends why he was going to abandon his new career, he found himself answering:

"It's too passive. I feel like I'm sitting on the sidelines."

His health was fast improving, and this, combined

with intellectual vigor, caused a craving for fulfilment of another kind—action, participation! But in what sphere? Anyhow Jack left Europe and resigned from his position as a reporter for the International News Service.

Home again, his father still carefully refrained from handing out advice. Still, a political situation existed in Boston that could not be ignored. Not that anyone suggested the possibility of Jack's *caring*, but there *was* a Congressional vacancy in the Eleventh District, due to the fact that James Michael Curley, long a political enemy of both of Jack's grandfathers, was giving up his seat in Congress to become the mayor of Boston. The Eleventh District covered East Boston, where both Jack's parents had been born, and also took in Cambridge, where the boys had gone to Harvard. More, this area included the strongly Irish sections of Brighton, Somerville and Charlestown, where the Kennedy name carried great weight.

One evening, before Jack was fully aware that his decision had been made, he suddenly found himself blurting out at the table:

"I think maybe I can win that election."

"What election?" Eunice asked, all innocence.

"Jim Curley's seat in Congress," Jack replied.

"Congress!" Ted shouted. "That's almost as good as being coach at Harvard."

"Almost," Robert put in dryly, and then asked, "When did you make up your mind, Jack?"

Jack grinned, shrugged, and told his brother truthfully, "I'm not quite sure. It just grew up in me, like Topsy."

Vainly trying to hide his pleasure, their father asked, "Are you sure this is what you want, Jack? Boston politics can be pretty dirty business."

"You're not trying to discourage me, are you, Dad?"

"You know better than that."

Even if he had wanted to, Jack would have had a terrible time backing out. All at once everyone was shouting, giving advice, offering help.

"I'll need all the assistance I can get," Jack said. "Grandfather Fitz will have to tutor me."

He recalled the time he had toured the wards with Honey Fitz, the skill of the old politician in charming with his blarney, laying it on the line, alternating between cajolery and threat. For the fraction of a second, John wondered if he could make the grade. By nature he was no politician, but it suddenly came to him that there were many ways to win. Boston politics had become extremely corrupt, the party bosses skilled in double-dealing. Why should he not play the game according to *his* lights?

"What are you thinking, John?" his mother asked.

She was intuitive, could sense a conflict, and Jack grinned.

"Thinking about ways to buck the bosses," he said.

He expected this to bring warnings from his father about the importance of winning over the old-time pros. Instead Joe, Sr. threw back his head and laughed, in the first real release from memory of his loss.

"If looks count," he said, "you've got a good start in playing it your own way."

"What's wrong with my looks?" Jack demanded.

If Kick had been there, she would probably have

told him, "You look like a scarecrow." Jack did. Still painfully thin, his skin yellowed from the atabrine pills he was taking to stave off a recurrence of malaria, he could not have less resembled the average well-fed politician.

Almost choking with laughter, Eunice said, "And your manners, Jack—you've got to unmend your manners."

"What do you mean by that?" her brother demanded.

"You're too polite," she said. "Besides, sometimes your speech sounds positively British."

"Decent diction didn't hurt FDR," Jack said.

"True," his father put in. "But Harry Truman's Missouri drawl isn't going to put the people against him either—except for the snobs. What Eunice is trying to say, John, is you're not exactly the poor man's political image."

"Maybe not, but sometimes it's good for people to have their image changed."

"Jack's right," their mother agreed. "There's no reason why politicians can't be gentlemen."

"That's true, Rose," her husband said. "But it's better sometimes not to show it."

Jack knew that his father was handing out small, practical hints which would stand him in good stead. However, he wasn't touching the real crux of the matter, was skirting the truth that Jack had not shown himself a good mixer. Still, he thought, his crew on the island had looked up to him, put their full confidence in his leadership. And he hadn't let them down.

He grinned and, adopting the tones of a gangster, asked, "Are you guys and gals tryin' to bust me out before I even get my foot in the door?"

"No, no," sounded in chorus. They all knew Jack could make it; they'd all help, and this was just the first step.

Pat spoke up then in defense of her brother's looks.

"His leanness and pallor are fetching," she said. "He has a sort of Cary Grant expression."

This evoked raised eyebrows from her mother, who commented dryly, "You're too impressed with movie stars, Pat."

"Bosh!" her daughter replied. "They play at fun, but we have it."

This may have been her opinion at the time, but she was later to marry Peter Lawford, handsome screen star.

There was more teasing, with mention being made that Jack—who detested hats—might have to buy himself a derby—and hang around bars—and get slapped on the back.

"If they wallop you hard, you'll cave in," Ted said.

This conversation ended with Jack chasing his youngest brother. Catching up with him, he said, "Let's see now who'll cave in." But he released the struggling Ted—didn't want to be the one to dominate.

When Jack first announced his candidacy for Congress, the hard-boiled ward heelers and political hangers-on wouldn't have given him a "Chinaman's chance" to win. In the first place, he was practically a stranger in the district, although both his grandfathers had once held office and controlled the votes

there. Honey Fitz was still living in retirement at the
Bellview Hotel, adjacent to the State House on Beacon
Hill. At eighty-three, John F. Fitzgerald was still vitally
and keenly interested in all that went on in Boston.
Indeed his quarters were a political hangout. If his
namesake didn't exactly fit the picture of a typical
hard-boiled candidate, Honey himself did the unusual
by keeping his politics on a very high level for one of
his time.

"Don't sell yourself short, Johnny; I'll help all I
can," the old man said. But he must often have been
dismayed by his grandson's refusal to play ball with
old and seasoned politicos. To Honey Fitz these repre-
sented the backbone of any organization, without
whose assistance one could not possibly win.

The Eleventh District was mainly peopled by the
poor, and included immigrants from every part of
the world. The slum area was as bad as any in the
nation and, as a by-product of misery, the crime rate
was exceedingly high. Saloons did a flourishing business for those who wished to forget the monotony of
factory work, deaden the sickening odor from the
dumps, and drown out the constant mumble of trains
in freight yards nearby.

This was strictly a Democratic party district, and
the voters were accustomed to tough-talking cohorts
of James Curley, who could speak their own language.
Thus the shy, soft-spoken son of Harvard, trying to
crack the shell of long-established rules, became a
target of ridicule for big bosses.

This Jack came to know, but faced with challenge,
his chin became more firmly set. If he could command

a PT boat, and plan a strategy to save most of his crew, he could at least campaign with the same determination. What if he didn't have Joe's outgoing, easy way with people? He would cover more streets, shake hands with more voters, and present himself to people whom politicians had never bothered about before. A friend, Dave Powers, who had worked for Kennedy in the Charlestown area, later said, "He didn't realize how surprised and how impressed those poor people were to find him knocking at their doors. Nobody else had ever taken the trouble to come to them."

He even amazed Joe, Sr., who, after watching his son shaking hands and asking for votes on a street corner in Maverick Square, said, "I never thought Jack had it in him."

Little by little, Jack built up confidence, and as time went on he lost his apologetic air and became convinced he had a chance to win. Even more, he realized that this was the kind of participation he had been craving, an outward expression of his interest in the arts of politics and social science. The day-to-day speculation about the strategy of rival candidates, speech writing, and endless activity in his busy campaign headquarters proved a source of constant excitement.

The primary race in which Jack was running engaged nine other Democratic candidates. In this district a Republican had no chance to win. His opponents, who played the game strictly as outlined by Curley's pros, at first regarded "the poor little rich boy's" strategy as a kind of three-ringed circus. What good did he think it would do to have a bunch of amateurs eager and ready to help? When Grandfather Fitz brought in wise old professional politicians, they quickly retreated from the well-bred conversational planning of "kids without know-how."

Some of these helpers were old friends from Harvard and Choate, like Torb Macdonald, Ted Reardon and LeMoyne Billings. Paul Fay, a friend from his PT boat squadron, flew from San Francisco to give Jack a hand. Then, there were those recently mustered out of service who were still at loose ends about choosing civilian careers. Was not Jack Kennedy a veteran hero whose brother died fighting for his country? He was young, could understand youth's problems.

Indeed, Jack would always retain a boyish zeal and charm which would make him a symbol of change in a world where those who clung to the past wishfully and wrongly pretended there had been no change. Even if Jack's speeches sounded mild and stuffy to politicians of the ranting school, he knew firsthand what had happened—world war, misery, displacement and insecurity. For those who had stayed at home while young men fought and died, his words may not have had much meaning when he said:

> Each passing day brings to light the increased need for prompt and intelligent action in public service. Veterans are daily faced with new problems of employment, housing and rehabilitation. The general public's needs are greater now than perhaps at any time in our nation's history. The demands

of peace are more far-reaching and more complete than the problems of the recent war.

"Highfalutin' " and far too general to pull in votes, was the general reaction of his opponents to such speeches. Still they had to admit Jack was working hard, popping in and out of grocery stores, bars, beauty shops, factories, and more and more speaking in the language of those whom he addressed of the need for jobs, the rising cost of living, decent housing, Social Security and medical care. Besides, he must have mesmerized the bunch of Ivy Leaguers working for him; they started early in the morning and didn't let up till midnight!

What his opponents didn't know was that nothing drove Jack Kennedy so hard as challenge, that their mud-slinging tactics served only to ripen him into a seasoned campaigner. He could neither be bought nor scared, could play both their game and his own. Before long he was eating spaghetti with Italians in the district, charming Chinese with his clumsy handling of chopsticks, speaking the same terse language as longshoremen, and listening to problems of mothers and housewives.

This was absurd; the skinny kid was getting somewhere—so lay on the smear thick, boys. It was easy to plant hecklers in an audience, who at the proper time would call out:

"Do you think your old man's millions can buy up this election?"

It would have been stupid to deny that his father

had helped finance the campaign, so Jack replied to such taunts in calm, cool tones:

"Sure my campaign cost money . . . but I mean to win on my own merits. . . . By the way, where did the boss who hired you to heckle get his funds?"

Meanwhile, Joe, Sr. was watching from the sidelines as his family once again worked as a team. Eunice answered phones, organized and suggested appeals to women voters. Bobby pounded the streets, took over wards and reinforced his brother's chances by smiling, gentlemanly Kennedy visits. More than anything, Jack's change from a shy young man to a seasoned campaigner who plotted and analyzed his course, astounded his father. Now that the primary day drew near, he added a suggestion of his own.

"One professional touch will clinch your chances," he told his son. "Though you'd probably win anyhow."

"What do you have in mind?" Jack asked.

"Add Frank Morrissey to your staff as campaign manager," his father suggested. "He knows the ropes like nobody in this town."

Jack accepted his father's advice, and Morrissey became his friend and manager for many years to come.

It was probably Morrissey, with an eye to public relations, who suggested that an article about Jack's wartime experiences in the Pacific be given wide circulation. This was a stirring account of the Lieutenant's heroism written by John Hersey for *The New Yorker* and later reprinted in the *Reader's Digest*.

By now Jack's opponents were so uneasy about his relentless door-to-door coverage of the district and the never-ending efforts of his staff, that they were almost afraid to laugh when learning about the "Kennedy teas." What next! Some did permit themselves the luxury of a sneer in speaking of these events.

Actually, these social get-togethers proved a great success. They gave the women constituents in the Eleventh District a chance to decide for themselves what Rose Kennedy and her girls were like. They had all heard about the daughter of John Fitzgerald, what a devout and good woman she was and not given to airs in the old days. Still, the family had moved away, and what with her husband being an ambassador—to say nothing about his millions—it would be interesting to see what the lot of them were like.

Doubters must have been astonished, because both Rose Kennedy and her daughters were naturally gracious, friendly people. Just women, like us, was the general impression. Couldn't have treated us better if we'd grown up together.

Jack won the nomination which assured him a seat in Congress by a larger margin than any backer had predicted. He had received more votes than the combined number of his nearest rivals, and twice as many as the man who came in second. When reporters asked his opinion about the reason for this large majority, Jack said:

"Timing means almost everything in politics. I was elected because I was the only veteran in the race, and if my brother Joe hadn't been killed he would have been the Congressman."

Of course he also gave credit to his loyal staff, and acknowledged his own hard work.

On the night of his victory old Honey Fitz climbed up on a table in his namesake's headquarters and sang, "Sweet Adeline."

Later, in a story about John Fitzgerald Kennedy as a leading presidential candidate, Bill Johnson, Boston correspondent for *Time* magazine, recalled the night of the 1946 primary. He wrote:

"That was the last real touch of traditional Boston Irish-American politics in the career of Jack Kennedy, the most phenomenally successful Irish-American politician of them all."

True, in his later career the Congressman-to-be chose as advisers a group of vigorous young intellectuals like his Presidential assistant, Ted Sorensen. But on that night of his nomination, Jack's and a chorus of well-bred Ivy League voices lustily joined in "Sweet Adeline" and, merging with Honey Fitz and his cronies, sang "In all my dreams, your fair face beams," and on, and on.

11

✫✫✫✫✫✫

THE YOUNG SENATOR

ALTHOUGH THE YOUNG CONGRESSMAN was twenty-nine,
he was often mistaken for a college student. He became accustomed to being called "laddie" by one of
the elder statesmen, and treated with tolerant,
fatherly affection by many members of the House. He
didn't mind looking young so long as his views were
taken seriously. And, Jack thought, as he mounted
the steps of the House, he had already caused moments of shocked surprise among his colleagues.

In the lobby he saw his friend George Smathers
from Florida, talking to a group of Representatives.
One of them spied the young Congressman from
Massachusetts, said something to his companions; and
they turned toward him, amused. George left the
group and came over to him.

"Are you taking the day off, Jack?" he questioned.

"No, why do you ask?"

"No reason," George Smathers told him.

This did not seem likely, but Jack did not press the point.

Smathers changed the subject, saying, "I got us theater tickets for that musical next week, Jack. It's supposed to be quite good."

He and George often double-dated. What a handsome, well-put-together fellow Smathers was! But why was he now grinning like a Cheshire cat?

"Don't wear sneakers to the theater, Jack," his friend was saying. "The young ladies mightn't like it."

"Roger! See you," Jack replied, then turned and hurried down the corridor.

He and George had high-spirited fun together as fellow bachelors. Both sometimes spoke of marriage, saying how sad it was thus far they had felt no urge to settle down. As ambitious young men on Capitol Hill, their plans were so centered on political problems that, as they jestingly assured one another, there wasn't time left for a serious courtship.

Jack ducked into the elevator, which was empty except for a timid-looking little man. He smiled and seemed relieved when Jack got in.

"Would you please leave me off at the fourth floor," he requested.

What *was* this? First, the group in the lobby had gazed at him in amusement; then Smathers had made that pointed remark about not wearing sneakers on their date; and now, this white rabbit stranger was treating him like an elevator operator. Still, Jack played the part and pushed the fourth floor button.

On his own floor, Jack hurried down the hall and

dashed into the rear door of his inner office. Impatiently he buzzed for his secretary, Mary Davis, who appeared at once.

"Look me over, will you," Jack said, "and tell me why I'm being high-hatted this morning?"

She scanned his clothes and said, "Well, Mr. Kennedy, I—I really don't know—"

Obviously she did and wasn't going to say.

"Many people there?" Jack asked, gesturing toward the outer office.

"Quite a few," she told him. "Mr. Reardon has been talking to them—here's a list of their names."

Mary handed him a typed list.

"I'll study it," Jack said, "but first tell Ted I want to see him, will you?"

Ted Reardon would pull no punches. Now Jack's administrative assistant, he had been Joe's best friend at Harvard, and in their present relationship Ted treated the Congressman more as a younger brother than as a boss. While waiting, Jack rubbed a hand over his cheek, thinking he might have forgotten to shave. This was a rite he performed absent-mindedly, often stroking away at his beard as he read a book propped up before him. His devoted housekeeper, Margaret Ambrose, learning about this habit, threatened to tell Jack's mother the next time she stopped by in Georgetown to see how her son was faring. He had solemnly promised the housekeeper to mend his ways, since she refused to accept the truth of the "safety" in safety razors!

Ted Reardon poked his head through the door, not seeming to notice anything unusual.

"There're quite a few people waiting to see you, Jack," he said.

"Yes, I've memorized the list. Just give me a rundown on who's who." Then he rose suddenly and added, "First, though, tell me—is there anything wrong with the way I look? I've been getting disapproving glances all morning."

"Want it straight?"

"Of course."

"Well," Ted said, "you look like you had crawled from under a rock. How did George Thomas let you get away with wearing that suit to the office?"

Jack gazed down at his trousers, which were indeed extremely rumpled; in addition he spied a large spot on the lapel of his coat. Surely this could not be the suit that his valet, George Thomas, had put out for him that morning!

"I must have made some mistake," Jack said.

Then he dismissed the subject and listened attentively as Ted briefed him on the people who waited in the outer office and the reasons they had come. After this, Jack was ready to deal with his callers' requests for jobs, complaints, and pleas to use his influence in settling special problems that had arisen in the State of Massachusetts, or in connection with other issues.

Around one o'clock George Thomas arrived with a large heated receptacle containing the Congressman's lunch. This was sent him daily by Margaret Ambrose in the hope she could put a little flesh on her gangly charge. Ted accompanied the valet into the inner chamber, and after Jack's luncheon was set out on his desk, he turned to George Thomas and teased:

"Did the Congressman sleep in his suit last night?" he asked.

The valet's expression was both disapproving and sad.

"Now, Mr. Ted," he explained, "it's not my fault Mr. Jack came to work dressed like that. I had that suit set aside to go to the cleaner's, but he grabs the first thing he finds."

"I *am* sorry, George," Jack said. "I was reading a whale of a good mystery while I dressed, and didn't notice what I was putting on."

If Jack's indifference to what he wore caused amusement among his colleagues, some of the older Representatives were just as critical of many of his attitudes. Who did the young Congressman think he was, refusing to play ball with the party machine? In their opinion, only a rash, inexperienced young man would dare to stand up as he did to John W. McCormack, longtime leader of the Massachusetts Democratic delegation. Didn't Kennedy know which side his bread was buttered on?

During his three terms in the House, Jack departed more and more from the political school of his grandfathers Patrick and Honey Fitz, whose first and unyielding devotion was to their party. But times had changed, and although it would be stupid to ignore the party leaders, the people themselves had become more politically aware and no longer followed the bosses blindly.

Jack considered first the wishes of the people who

had sent him to the House to represent them. He favored rent control and labor reform measures, and he fought the Taft-Hartley Act which restricted labor unions. Occasionally he risked displeasing powerful interests, if the cause he was fighting for seemed worthwhile.

This was especially true when a low-cost housing bill was introduced in Congress. He gave it his support, for during his campaign he had seen the misery of people living in the slums—hollow-eyed children, so undernourished that their schoolwork suffered and they seemed stupid simply because they were hungry. And he had visited overcrowded tenements where people shivered from lack of heat in winter, and in summer were stifled by the stench from factory fumes and dumps. He had also been moved by the plight of those veterans who had fought for their country, and on returning could find no jobs. Many who had served in the armed forces were still living in damp basements and rat-infested buildings.

Jack went all out for the low-cost housing bill, not only in Congress but when he was campaigning in Massachusetts. Curiously enough, the American Legion was siding with those who opposed this Federal aid to housing. At a meeting of the Veterans of Foreign Wars, held in Boston, Jack took his stand against those who allied themselves with wealthy realtors, and introduced a resolution supporting the bill before Congress. Later, when he was speaking in support of the bill in the House, he was reminded from the floor that the powerful American Legion did not share his views. Jack said:

"I am a member of the American Legion. . . . I was never consulted." Here he lost his temper—which rarely happened—and added, "The leadership of the American Legion has not had a constructive thought for the benefit of the country since 1918!"

The shock caused by this statement made many of Jack's advisers fear that his popularity would suffer from the use of such strong words. But it didn't turn out that way. Approved by the smaller veteran's groups and labor, his stand reflected the wishes of more voters than if he had sided with those who opposed the bill.

Jack's early Congressional career was marked by a sad event. In May 1948, his sister Kathleen was killed in an airplane accident. Her huband's family, the Cavendishes, who had come to love her as though she had been their own daughter, grieved deeply. One British nobleman paid this tribute to the Marchioness: "We thought she was the best thing America ever sent to England."

Jack's sorrow was more personal. It was almost impossible to believe that his dearly beloved Kick was gone.

During his three terms as Congressman, Jack's colleagues found it difficult to pin a label on him. Although his votes were for the most part "liberal," he did not hesitate to criticize labor if he felt its demands were unfair. Indeed, it was Jack's habit of examining both sides of each issue that caused many people to think he was cold or indifferent. This was not so. As always, he wanted the facts before he tried to arrive at an impartial judgment. For instance, although he accused the Labor Committee of not understanding the problems of the workers, he also attacked labor leaders for not permitting free speech in their unions.

He was equally impartial in regard to foreign affairs, weighing each situation in the light of Cold War conditions. He did not hesitate to criticize the Truman administration, and even placed blame on Roosevelt for having been too soft with Stalin in agreements made after the war. Now it appeared that American ground troops would have to be sent to Western Europe as a safeguard against possible future Soviet attack. To this the Congressman agreed, but when he suggested that Europeans should supply six divisions for every division sent from America, some of Jack's enemies accused him of being "an isolationist, like his father."

If Congressman Kennedy had critics, he served his State so well that Jack knew he could keep his seat in the House indefinitely. This, he now decided, was not where he wanted to stay.

Not exactly certain of what office he wished to seek, Jack nonetheless decided to campaign in his State of Massachusetts. In 1948, he considered running for the Senate against Leverett Saltonstall, but on weighing what he believed to be his chances, he decided against it. In 1951, he considered taking a chance on another plane.

In the spring of that year, Jack was invited to a dinner party at the home of a newspaperman, Charles Bartlett, and his wife Martha. Here he found himself seated next to a beautiful and charming young lady named Jacqueline Lee Bouvier.

"My friends called me Jackie," she told the Congressman. "And I hope you will, too."

Jack flashed her a smile, and that evening he asked her for a date.

She told him, yes, she would like that very much, and soon after this attractive couple was seen a few times dining out together.

In his orderly way of putting "first things first," Jack displayed his interest in Jackie in much the same way he went about gathering statistics. He learned that she had been born in Southampton, Long Island, and had attended the finest girls' schools: Miss Chapin's in New York, Holton Arms in Washington, Miss Porter's school in Connecticut. But this was not all: she had studied two years at Vassar and a year at the Sorbonne in Paris, where she had majored in eighteenth-century European history. Now that she was completing her education at George Washington University in the capital, she told Jack that she hoped soon to embark on some career.

Seated across a table one evening Jack said, "One thing you forgot to mention was winning the *Vogue* Prix de Paris contest. How did it happen you didn't take the position they offered in their Paris office? I thought a job in Paris was every woman's dream."

"I guess I was afraid to go," Jackie told him. "After that year at the Sorbonne, I felt that if I went back I'd stay there forever—I loved Paris so much. And then I knew I really ought to finish up my college work."

It seemed amazing to him that the shy, soft-spoken Jacqueline was so fond of learning, but he hastened to assure her that *he* was glad of the decision she had made.

She urged him then to talk about himself, and sat listening wide-eyed as he spoke of his special interests—of his taste for books of American history, his admiration for men who had shown courage in upholding their convictions. And he spoke about his family—somehow the thought of Kathleen kept coming into his mind.

Adept at hiding his feelings, Jack made his voice sound casual when he said, "In some ways you are like her, Jackie. The kind of girl one remembers."

For the next year, though, he risked giving the impression that she was the kind of girl that one forgot, and Jackie herself went on to other things.

In 1952 Governor Paul Dever of Massachusetts, a Democrat, decided not to run for the Senate against the Republican candidate, Henry Cabot Lodge. The Governor considered his chances of winning far too slim, for Lodge was a real vote-getter and he would be running on a Republican ticket headed by the World War II hero, General Dwight D. Eisenhower.

At this point Congressman Kennedy decided to move in on the situation, for he had long wanted something bigger than his post in the House. It was much easier for a Senator to become a national figure than for a Congressman.

"Do you think we can win?" he asked his brother

Robert, using the "we" because this battle would require the combined efforts of the family "team."

"What do you mean, do I *'think* we can win'?" his brother demanded. "Of course we can."

"Paul Dever thought the job was too tough for him," Jack reminded him.

"Well, it's not too tough for us," Robert said.

Jack grinned and added, "Since you're so sure of yourself, how would you like to be my campaign manager?"

"Who else?"

This was the attitude of the Kennedys. Soon the clan was together again. The brothers and sisters spurred one another on to greater and greater efforts, and Jack himself campaigned in three hundred and fifty-one cities and towns of Massachusetts. Once again the political pros were amused at the idea that a "bunch of youngsters," who seemed to spring up like mushrooms all over the place, thought they could put their man in. Imagine a campaign manager aged twenty-seven! But Bobby was earnest, energetic. Get to work! Every minute counts! were his watchwords to Jack's helpers.

If Jack was busy in one part of the State, Robert would show up to fill his place. If *he* was busy, there were always Jean and Eunice and Pat to ring doorbells and charm women voters with their gracious interest. Old politicos who forgot the success of the "Kennedy teas" when Jack had run for Congressman, again joked slyly about the "three-ring circus" when invitations were sent out for Kennedy receptions. When these gatherings drew fifty thousand women to drink tea and chat with the Kennedys, these affairs were shown on national TV circuits. Those who had been present would tell their friends, and they, their friends, of the way Rose Kennedy had spoken up on behalf of her son. All knew that this Gold Star mother's own father was the genial John Fitzgerald, once the mayor of Boston.

Beyond these social get-togethers, there were other important factors working in Jack's behalf. In the first place, the family contributed heavily to the campaign, and since Lodge had accepted the post of Eisenhower's campaign manager, he had less time to stump for himself in Massachusetts. Then, too, Adlai Stevenson, the Democratic nominee for President running against General Eisenhower, referred to the young Congressman as "my kind of guy."

When the votes were finally counted, the Republicans had won by a national landslide, and swept in members of their party running for every office in Massachusetts—with one exception. John Fitzgerald Kennedy was the victor over Henry Cabot Lodge by 70,000 votes.

When he returned to Washington as Senator, at thirty-six, Jack started again on another campaign— the courtship of Jacqueline Bouvier. And in all the many languages she spoke, Jacqueline said "yes" when he proposed.

The marriage took place in 1953, in St. Mary's Roman Catholic Church at Newport, Rhode Island.

Six hundred guests attended, and thousands of towns-people from surrounding areas crowded close to get a glimpse of the popular young Senator and his bride. Archbishop Richard J. Cushing celebrated the nuptial Mass and read a special blessing from the Pope. More than twelve hundred persons were invited to the reception at Hammersmith Farm, the beautiful estate of the bride's mother and stepfather.

Senator and Mrs. John Kennedy spent their honeymoon in Acapulco, a sun-drenched garden spot on the Pacific coast of Mexico. Their future life would have to be different from this carefree interlude of fun and love, Jack told his beautiful bride. Of course. She was no child, even though she sometimes did enjoy leaning on her husband. Still, she told him, she was stronger than her image might suggest.

"And you can always count on me when the chips are down, Jack," she promised.

With her kind of steadfastness, he knew this to be so.

They chose for a home a large, gracious, rambling house in Virginia, which seemed an ideal spot to bring up children. There, Jackie could ride and paint and dream in privacy, but what she wanted was to be nearer her husband. Jack's senatorial duties became increasingly demanding, so his wife suggested buying a house in Georgetown. This charming section of Washington was quiet and pleasant; besides, it took her husband only a short while to come home.

In subtle ways the two came more and more to influence one another, she by perfecting her knowledge of subjects close to him, and he by enlarging the scope of his interests. Jacqueline became an avid reader of American history, and often translated foreign documents for her husband. He became more appreciative of symphonic music and the arts, and even tried his hand at sketching.

Jacqueline's beauty and brains, plus her gift for entertaining, made her in the public eye "a prize." With exquisite taste in every area, her dinner parties were as decorative and gracious as the charming hostess. Nods of approval conveyed the belief that she was an extremely valuable asset to her husband.

She was, but their time of full happiness would have to wait, because the past caught up and cast a shadow on the present. The Senator's back, which he had strained severely while campaigning, started to trouble him again. By an act of sheer will, he had managed to conceal his pain, hoping the condition would improve. Instead he grew steadily worse and, at the insistence of Jacqueline and his family, he sought the advice of many specialists. A spinal fusion was suggested, but some of the doctors believed that the operation would carry grave risks. The final verdict was that the Senator himself must make the decision. Jack did. What determined him were the crutches he had been forced to use for several months. He could not tolerate dependence on these wooden props.

"I'd rather die than go through life with them," was his firm comment on this subject.

"I want to go through with this," he told Jackie. "You're with me, aren't you?"

Torn with anxiety and wanting to plead against the choice, she nevertheless smiled, and told him quietly, "Of course I'm with you, Jack. All the way—always."

At her husband's side during the long weeks that followed, she was able to give the appearance of remaining calm. That the operation was indeed serious was confirmed by the fact that twice Jack was given the last rites of the Church. After this first operation, full cure still seemed extremely questionable, but the young couple were permitted to spend Christmas with Jack's family at Palm Beach.

But by the middle of February, he was back in the hospital for another operation. With him, whenever permitted, was his wife, her rounded cheeks now thinning with tension.

"I know it won't be as bad this time," she told him with false gaiety. "I feel it in my bones."

She was right, for the second bout of surgery did prove easier and more successful than the first. The surgeons now held out hope that Jack would eventually be able to move about freely. Of course, he would have to stay on his back in the hospital for months, but, in thankfulness, Jackie asked:

"What do a few months matter?"

During Jack's convalescence, his thoughts turned more and more to his ideal of courage. To forget his terrible pain, he read many biographies of famous Americans—his favorite subject. He decided to write a book about certain statesmen, whose spirit of gallantry he much admired. In this work, *Profiles in Courage,* he stated the belief that courage can be shown equally by opponents, that reasonable and thinking men can hold to their convictions. The book was dedicated to his wife, and he said:

This book could not have been possible without the encouragement, assistance and criticism offered me from the very beginning by my wife, Jacqueline, whose help during all my days of convalescence I cannot ever adequately acknowledge.

When she spoke of the courage Jack himself had shown during those terrible months of suffering, he smiled and denied he merited the term.

"You were the one who was a tower of strength, Jackie," he said.

"No," she protested. "I'm all jelly inside."

"Never say that again," he objected. "As you once said, you always come through when the chips are down."

"I hope I always will," she told him.

Jack's back continued to trouble him for some months after his release from the hospital, but he was again in Washington in May of 1955. Many of his colleagues had followed his progress during the long ordeal, and the day he made his first appearance in the Senate after his return, all the members stood up and applauded him as one man.

In 1956, when *Profiles in Courage* was published by Harper & Brothers, it became at once a best seller, and no one was amazed when it was awarded the Pulitzer Prize. More and more attention was focussed on the young Senator from Massachusetts.

Jack was now back in his usual round of political campaigning, for in Massachusetts a fight was going on within the Democratic party for control of the State committee. He traveled back and forth, making speeches and organizing his forces against strong opposition. He won out, and emerged in control of the 16 votes which Massachusetts would cast in the National Democratic Convention to be held in August of that year.

One morning, as he was shaving, he suddenly thrust his book away. His face in the mirror seemed to be trying to tell him something. What? Before the words were formed, an objection came. It was as if a chorus of challenging voices were saying, "But no Catholic has ever been President of the United States."

He slicked back his hair, grinned, and asked the reflection, "Why not? Is this attitude American?" Why should he not think in that direction? Perhaps if he were to be nominated for the Vice Presidency—maybe, later...

When the convention assembled at Chicago's International Amphitheater, Senator Kennedy learned that Adlai Stevenson wanted him to make the nominating speech in his behalf. Jack and Ted Sorensen spent the night working on the speech, and so effective was it that Stevenson won on the first ballot.

The nomination for the Vice Presidency was then thrown open to the convention, and although for a time the prospects seemed bright for Jack Kennedy, in the end he lost to Senator Estes Kefauver of Tennessee. But this, the first defeat of his political career, became a steppingstone to future victory. All the country had seen the handsome, gracious young man, heard him ask that his opponent's nomination be made unanimous. John Fitzgerald Kennedy had become a national figure.

As time went on, Jack came to feel that he had perhaps been fortunate in losing the vice-presidential nomination in 1956, for the Democratic candidates were roundly defeated at election time by Eisenhower and Nixon. His own political record was intact, and his star continued to rise.

In November 1957, he and Jackie had particular cause for thanksgiving when their little daughter Caroline was born. "With the way women are going places these days," Jack said jovially to the young mother, "there's no reason she can't be President when she grows up."

There was no doubt now of the goal Jack Kennedy had in mind. He knew the strikes against him. First there was his religion—it was generally believed that no Catholic could rise to the highest political and social position in the nation. Then many would hold his youth against him, believing that only age and long experience in national and international affairs would qualify a man to lead the country in such times.

Jack was aware of all these things that day as he rejoiced with Jackie over the birth of their first child. Suddenly, his mood became serious. In this world where the twilight of a Cold War could last for years, what a terrible responsibility to be President! Suddenly the shrill wail of his infant daughter filled him with sadness for helpless, hungry children everywhere. This should be a better world for innocents. A President must have a heart as well as reason.

12

☆☆☆☆☆☆

"LET US BEGIN"

ON THAT DAY of January 20, 1961, the Capitol dome cut a white silhouette in the cloudless sky as a northwest wind rattled against the stands set up for the ceremonies. Caught by the force, the red, white, and blue bunting fluttered and puffed out, and the people seated on the wooden benches sank deeper into heavy overcoats. They seemed almost motionless except for clouds of steam coming from their lips as warm breath struck the bitter cold.

Against this scene, bleached white by winter sun, the formal clothes of the dignitaries were like coal-black cutouts. High silk hats were the order of the day for an Inauguration, and the man who at any moment now would become America's youngest President had his slanted at a slightly rakish angle. Doubtless, before leaving the house in Georgetown, he had made some humorous reference to this headgear and was chided by his wife.

"Just once, Jack," she probably said, "please don't look like someone *forced* you to cover your hair."

Not that she wanted to share the limelight, but, hoping Jack would also be proud of her, the Senator's lady could well have asked:

"How do you like *my* costume?"

And he, "It looks O.K. to me."

He little suspected, nor did she, that Jacqueline's style—the pillbox hat, the bouffant hairdo and understated clothes—would alter the trend of women's fashions for years all over the world.

The Marine Band, vivid in bright colors and with regimental ribbons fluttering in the breeze, blared forth, "America the Beautiful." The familiar strains might have tempted many to join in and sing lustily to dispel the cold, but one dared not at such a solemn time. Dwight Eisenhower, the outgoing President and Commander in Chief, who had served as leader of the Armed Forces in World War II, sat smiling genially. His duty well done, he had used his popularity and prestige to help nominate the Republican candidate, Richard Nixon. But Dick had lost, and, although "Ike" must have felt disappointment, his first hopes were as always for the country's good. The contest was over; the reins of government were changing hands; this was Democracy.

At 12:21 a figure moved to the podium, and the presiding officer solemnly declared:

"We are here to inaugurate the thirty-fifth President of this free people."

John Kennedy stood up as a blast of fanfares shattered the silence. Why did he pause before pro-

ceeding forward to the place where Chief Justice Earl
Warren stood waiting. Of all reasons: to remove his
heavy topcoat!

If the cold winds had wafted voices from the past, a
mother would have said, "Sometimes, I don't know
what gets into him. What he's got against hats and
heavy coats I can't imagine."

Then the father, "Rose, you must not coddle them."

Now, Joe, Sr. sat weeping unashamedly with pride—
but his tears were also for the first son who had died
in battle. The mother, still quite unimpressed by what
mortal man calls success, wondered why Jack had
not been content to remain a Senator, and had so
flatly stated:

"He could have had a very interesting time in Washington as a Senator," she had told an astonished reporter.

Her son moved briskly now, coatless, hatless, and
his bushy forelock somewhat subdued by a very short
haircut. He raised his right hand, and, over a family
Douay Bible, pronounced the solemn words of office:

"I do solemnly swear. . ."

John Fitzgerald's Kennedy's Inaugural Address was
proclaimed a masterpiece. In clear confident tones he
spoke not only to the people of America, but sent out
a vigorous message of hope to peoples everywhere.

Let the word go forth from this time and place to
friend and foe alike, that the torch has been passed
to a new generation of Americans—born in this
century, tempered by war, disciplined by a cold and
bitter peace, proud of their ancient heritage—and

unwilling to witness or permit the slow undoing of those human rights to which this nation has always been committed, and to which we are committed to this day. . . .

Here, his clipped Boston speech sliced through the wind, his hands hammering against all doubters of his sincerity.

Let every nation know, whether it wish us well or ill, that we shall pay any price, bear any burden, meet any hardship, support any friend or oppose any foe in order to assure the survival and success of liberty.

This much we pledge—and more. . . .

Let us begin.

The Republicans had been pleased by the nomination of John Fitzgerald Kennedy. They considered his chances of winning very slim. Now, they said, if the opposition had put up a seasoned candidate like Lyndon Johnson, it would have been a different story. Kennedy was too young; besides, he was a Catholic. Totally disregarding the fact that their own nominee, Richard Nixon, was only three years older than the incumbent, they behaved as if Kennedy was still in a kiddy-car.

Viewing his chances with his usual reasonableness, Jack had known from the first that he had a tough fight on his hands. Win or lose, he made up his mind to try, and at an early date he assembled a vigorous young staff and began speaking engagements all over the country.

The most controversial national issue was civil rights, and specifically the second-class status of Negroes in the country. He could still hear the hue and cry of "Communist" directed toward the conservative Dwight D. Eisenhower for having sent troops into Little Rock, Arkansas, to quell riots by the segregationists. The Negroes' claim to the simple rights of equal citizenship seemed to affect the South as cause to fight another Civil War!

The Senator's advisers tried to dissuade him from going to the South, pointing out the political disadvantages of such a move. Should he try to pour balm on the wounds of Southern egos, he would alienate the liberals in the North. On the other hand, if he spoke out, in the fullness of belief, saying that "life, liberty and the pursuit of happiness" were intended for all, he could well lose the votes of Southerners and conservatives. A speaking engagement had been made for him in Mississippi long before the trouble in Little Rock, and the Senator had insisted upon going there. On his arrival, local newspapers had carried an article by the State's Republican chairman, daring Senator Kennedy to state his views on school integration.

Win or lose, there were issues which must be met head on and answered in a direct, unyielding manner. The rights of minorities were not merely of local concern, but direct challenges in a changing world. Did not the Fourteenth Amendment to our Constitution provide equal rights for all American citizens, regardless of color or race? And had not a Supreme Court decision declared segregation in the schools illegal?

Scrupulous in his belief in a government of law,

Jack had swung into this phase of the battle with assurance.

"I have no hesitancy in telling the Republican chairman," he said, "the same thing I told my own city of Boston. I accept the Supreme Court decision as the supreme law of the land. I think most of us agree on the necessity to uphold law and order in all parts of the country . . ." He paused then and blurted out, "And now I challenge the local Republican chairman to tell us where he stands on Eisenhower and Nixon!"

Actually, the programs of both parties had a liberal tone, but the Democrats called for greater government spending to speed up national growth and social reform. This, of course, became a target for the opposition.

Before audiences heady with confidence and expected victory, Richard Nixon had resorted to touches of humor. Where was the money coming from? he wanted to know.

"It's not Jack's money," he reminded admirers. "It's *yours.*"

As the momentum of the campaign increased, Senator Kennedy's Catholicism came more and more into the open as a cause of opposition to him. Hate literature of any kind, whether from the radical Right or from the Left, is alien to everything American, but again and again Jack's religion became an issue in the campaign, and vicious expressions of hate and prejudice appeared on the American scene. Many misinformed persons may have sincerely believed that Jack's Catholicism could threaten the American principle of separation of Church and State.

Most Protestant ministers had been wise enough to remain silent on this subject, but not all. Especially in the Midwest and South, some had openly preached from the pulpit that to elect a Catholic President would be courting national disaster. Against the counsel of some advisers, Jack took up this challenge also. As a counterthrust to misunderstanding and bigotry, he flew to Texas to address the Greater Houston Ministerial Association. To this group of clergymen, he said:

> Whatever issue may come before me as President, if I should be elected—I will make my decision in accordance with what my conscience tells me to be in the national interest, and without regard to outside religious pressure or dictates. And no power or threat of punishment could cause me to decide otherwise. But if the time should ever come—and I do not concede that any conflict would be even remotely possible—when my office would require me to either violate my conscience or violate the national interest, then I would resign from office, and I hope any conscientious public servant would do the same. . . .

In a series of television debates with Richard Nixon Jack had outshone his opponent in every way. His unruffled calm, his gift for getting to the heart of the matter and a flair for the dramatic, combined with good looks, made Nixon's attempts to defeat him ineffective.

Another incident that brought Jack votes was the arrest of Martin Luther King, the Negro leader, whose nonviolent efforts to raise the standards of his people would later be rewarded by a nomination for the Nobel Prize. In Atlanta, where King had been active in training Negroes to win their rights as citizens through peaceful measures, he was arrested on a minor traffic charge—and put in jail. This had given Senator Kennedy a chance to make it clear that the Democratic civil rights program meant what it said. He put in a personal call to Mrs. King, which was followed by another to an Atlanta judge by Robert Kennedy. Both expressed sympathy for the cause of Martin Luther King and approval of his efforts to attain long overdue rights for his people. Nixon, flirting with the Southern white vote, remained silent on this issue; this seemed not to have helped him in the South and caused him to lose the majority of Negro votes in Northern industrial areas.

One of the more subtle aspects of Jack's growing popularity could only be called the Kennedy appeal. Regardless of the time of his arrival, streets had been filled with milling throngs who broke through police lines to touch him, claw him and shake his hand. Though youth had seemed to form the backbone of his support, his tirelessness and genial, vigorous good looks acted as a magnet for every age and class.

Slowly his campaign had accelerated and spread, until its tempo seemed to defy time. Day and night he traveled at high speed, and at every stop was surrounded by shrieking, enthusiastic mobs.

Had the tide turned in his favor? *The New York Times,* frequently Republican in national elections, had in the end endorsed Senator Kennedy.

To offset the notion that Jack's growing popularity was based on the fickle whim of an admiring public, Walter Lippmann, dean of columnists, had written:

> . . . It has been truly impressive to see the precision of Mr. Kennedy's mind, his immense command of facts, his instinct for the crucial point, his singular lack of demagoguery and sloganeering, his intense concern and interest in the subject itself, the stability and steadfastness of his nerves and the coldness of his courage.

Still the opposition to him was real and strong. Although some had predicted that he would win by a landslide, it was actually the closest presidential race in this century.

But he had won—and, before taking office, had to select able advisers for his Cabinet. Again reason had guided him in the choices. Dean Rusk, president of the Rockefeller Foundation, had been named Secretary of State; Robert S. McNamara, president of the Ford Motor Company was to be Secretary of Defense; Adlai Stevenson, whose intellectual brilliance had not served him in the pursuit of the Presidency, had been named as the new Ambassador to the United Nations; a Republican, Douglas Dillon, whose love of America erased party lines, had been the choice for Secretary of the Treasury; Abraham Ribicoff, former Governor of Connecticut, would take his place in the Cabinet as Secretary of Health, Education and Welfare.

The naming of his brother Robert as Attorney General had caused the first outcry of "Kennedy dynasty."

But if the young President had not appointed his hard-working, able and patriotically devoted brother to the cabinet, the Commander in Chief would not have been named John Fitzgerald Kennedy.

A nation of TV viewers saw the new President as he took the oath of office, heard the ring of his voice as he made his Inaugural Address. By a simple turn of the switch they were transported to that stirring scene before the Capitol, and millions felt they had been present as history unfolded.

Those who watched and heard could understand that their President's "Let us begin" was his own burning desire to get things started, away from the thought of the Cold War that had held the world in bondage for so many years. He first reminded them that they could not permit "the slow undoing of those human rights to which this nation has always been committed," and that the nation would meet any price to assure liberty for all.

Next he pledged loyalty to our old Allies, and co-operation with them in new ventures for the common good. He welcomed into the ranks of free nations those countries just emerging from colonial rule, at the same time warning them of the dangers of replacing old tyrannies by new.

To the underprivileged all over the world he said:

To those people in huts and villages of half the globe struggling to break the bonds of mass misery, we pledge our best efforts to help them help themselves, for whatever period is required—not because the Communists are doing it, not because we seek their votes, but because it is right. If the free society cannot help the many who are poor, it can never save the few who are rich.

Especially to the Republics south of our border he offered a new Alliance for Progress to cast off the bonds of poverty, and a promise that the United States would join in opposing aggression anywhere in our hemisphere.

He expressed his belief in the United Nations as the logical body by which world peace should be upheld, and requested those nations who had made themselves our enemies to join us in renewing the quest for peace before the mutual threat of destruction by atomic war. To this end he called for serious proposals for inspection and control of arms, for joint effort in scientific research and space projects, for the stamping out of disease, for the encouragement of the arts and commerce—in short for a new world where law would prevail and peace be preserved.

It was then that he said:

All this will not be finished in the first 100 days. Nor will it be finished in the first 1,000 days, nor in the life of this administration, nor even perhaps in our lifetime on this planet. *But let us begin. . . .* And so, my fellow Americans: Ask not what your country will do for you—ask what you can do for your country. My fellow citizens of the world: Ask not what America will do for you, but what together we can do for the freedom of man.

The Kennedy administration had begun, and was soon marked by a breathless series of major events— the unsuccessful invasion of Cuba's Bay of Pigs, the Berlin Wall, riots in Mississippi and other places in the battle for civil rights, and the showdown with Russia over Cuba.

The United States had endorsed the efforts of the Cuban government-in-exile to overthrow the Communist dictatorship that had taken over their country. Although this was a problem John Kennedy had inherited from the previous administration, he acknowledged that he had made a wrong decision. Directly, and with no attempt to shift the blame, he said: "I assume full responsibility for this failure."

When it was discovered that Russia was placing in Cuba missiles with a range that could reach the United States, JFK declared a blockade of Cuba. Russian ships bound for that island were to be stopped, searched, and, if carrying armaments, turned back to their bases. Thus he risked war, which if it came and spread would surely involve the use of nuclear weapons. . . . Still, if by the push of a button, the Russians could blow America to smithereens, the same could be done to them. In spite of growls and threats, the Russian leaders had no intention of being wiped out for a small island halfway round the world. They backed down, and removed their offensive missiles.

If this was a high peak in the Kennedy administration, peace-loving peoples of the world rejoiced even more when America, Britain, and Russia finally agreed to ban all aboveground nuclear tests, and the treaty between them came into effect on October 10, 1963, with ceremonies in Washington, London, and Moscow.

Yet sometimes these great historic moments are not retained in the mind so vividly as more personal aspects of the lives of the First Family. . . . Caroline in her mother's high heeled shoes, interrupting an important meeting . . . Jackie, standing by her husband's side in South America, charming the people by addressing them in their native language. . . . Their second child, a son, born shortly after the election and called John-John by his father, because the President admitted that when he grew older he never cared for his nickname "Jack," and wished to emphasize that this first son's name was *John*. . . . The President's flair for style and flashes of humor when challenged at press conferences by questioners wishing to irritate. . . . His disregard for security measures, and eluding protectors to move in crowds at home and abroad, mobbed and besieged by admirers who seemed to believe that even to touch the vigorous, hatless, coatless man would bring them luck. . . . His visit to Ireland, where somehow the humble home of his ancestors seemed to twist his tongue into a brogue, and transport him into the sphere of goblins and leprechauns.

The Kennedys' short stay in the White House was not without personal tragedy. The President's vigorous father was reduced to helplessness by a stroke, and the infant son Patrick, prematurely born, could not be saved in spite of heroic efforts. It was a bowed and sorrowful father, who visited the grave of *his second son.*

It must have been a comfort to John Fitzgerald

Kennedy to receive the Sacraments of his Church, to
become as one with God and draw inspiration from
His peace. He must have also found comfort in the
teachings of another John, the good Pope John. As
leader of his Faith, the Pope had made known his
ideas on working Christianity. In his message "Peace
on Earth" he taught that, in reality, men must learn
to live together as brothers. He warned against
nationalism and pride as threats to the peace of the
world; he pointed out the danger of thermonuclear
war as the first problem in our times; he deplored the
plight of the poor and unemployed and declared that
this plight must be the concern of all who would call
themselves Christians.

It would be impossible to know what went on in
the mind of one so adept at putting up a front as JFK.
But by many outward indications he did reach that
peak of becoming as one with his people, with their
needs and welfare as his first cause. No longer was he
molded chiefly by the past, but the wave of the future.

Even the White House became a living heritage,
with Jacqueline as hostess explaining the plans for its
restoration. And as she did so, her graciousness suggested that she was merely showing the people what
in reality belonged to them.

There was scarcely any phase of human welfare
to which the President's interest did not extend. He
pushed measures to provide for fundamental needs,
such as food, housing and shelter; he established the
Peace Corps and forwarded the causes of education
and physical fitness. And he established the National

Cultural Center to promote the performing arts—needless to say, Jackie had a hand in that!

The whole idea of John Kennedy's New Frontier was to sow the seeds of change, holding hope for future generations. Youth looked to JFK to understand their problems. His vigor and boyish smile created a sort of Pied Piper illusion for little children. Of the 20,000 letters received weekly at the White House, 2,000 were penned by boys and girls. Many chose to call their President "Jack," and did not hesitate to tell him how to run the country!

Despite his popularity, John Fitzgerald Kennedy also knew frustration and setbacks. The initial mistake in the Cuban crisis had been overcome by his final triumph, but there was still much sentiment against him in the South, and in Congress strong opposition to measures that lay close to his heart. Action was delayed again and again on his civil rights bill and on the tax cut he proposed to relieve unemployment, and his bill for foreign aid was slashed.

Although he knew from the beginning that he would not have time to accomplish his major objectives (had he not said, "All this will not be finished in the first 100 days. Nor will it be finished in the first 1,000 days, nor in the lifetime of this administration, nor even perhaps in our lifetime on this planet"?), he always seemed to feel a sense of urgency to get things done. It was almost as if the wheels of accomplishment grind too slowly when death could lurk close by. Still he could not have known, was willing to hold out a hand to haters, and flash a smile in order to convert them.

In the third year of President Kennedy's term in

office, the political parties again tested their strength for the election the following year. Hate took a more insidious form than usual, bursting into overt hostile action. Vice-President Johnson and his wife had been the victims of insults and violence because of their sympathetic attitude toward civil rights. Adlai Stevenson, on a visit to Dallas, Texas, had also been subjected to violence and smears by those who would do away with the United Nations. Even so, the President decided to undertake an unofficial political tour, to show himself again the vigorous campaigner, lest the people had forgotten. He laughed at Stevenson's warnings to keep away from Dallas, because John Kennedy refused to consider seriously the rumblings of radicals.

One can almost hear him:

"Oh, come now, my friend, you don't expect me to change my plans for a bunch of crackpots."

This was quite recklessly ignoring the paid advertisements of hate-mongers that appeared in Dallas newspapers prior to his visit there.

It was a day like any other day, with people going about their chores, amusements, household duties. All seemed well; the nation had seen on the screen their President's reception in Dallas, which had been no less warm in welcome than in the other states he had visited. Like a thunderbolt, the awful intelligence spread that the President had been shot. Incredible, beyond belief. Of course he had his enemies, but who would want to take the life of a genial young man, with a wife and children and family—and one who besides was *our President*. The news was confirmed.

Riding in the car with Governor John Connally, Mrs. Kennedy and Mrs. Connally, both men had been shot. Whether mortally was not yet known, but it would be—far too soon!

President John Fitzgerald Kennedy died in a Dallas hospital at 1:00 P.M., November 22, 1963. A priest hurried to the hospital to give him the last rites of the Roman Catholic Church.

The alleged assassin was a radical Leftist, who was shot to death before his trial; the radical Rightists were glad it had not been one of them. Haters did not halt, but all those in the world with hearts would never again be entirely without grief.

The next night in the Capitol rotunda three hundred thousand people paid mournful homage to their President. Throngs waited for hours in the chill of night, to be able to stop for a moment at the flag-draped bier and say farewell. Twice the widow had knelt there, numb, but she turned once toward the people—the people who had loved Jack.

Why did she think in the past tense? All this *could not be.*

But if the terrible thing was so, how to tell the children? She must, and so she did. Later the child Caroline knelt with her mother beside the flag-draped casket. Again, she and John-John were with their mother at the requiem Mass celebrated by Cardinal Cushing, who had married John and Jacqueline at what seemed but "a brief, shining moment" before. Three-year-old John-John, who had gone with his father on Veterans Day to the grave of the Unknown

Soldier at Arlington, thought it would be fitting to salute on this day, too, like a real soldier.

Always in the past, the mother, Jacqueline, had tried to protect her children against publicity. Not now, though. Their father, the President of the United States, had given his life for humanity. A great President, his funeral must reflect his greatness. Their children would remember the caisson, the muffled beat of drums, and the riderless horse. . . .

Images most vivid remain always in the mind. We see a woman walking, her face transformed into a stricken mask, but walking, walking. Her brother-in-law Robert on one side and flanked by other Kennedys, the total effect was of the kind of grief contained in a Greek tragedy. On and on to the grave in Arlington Cemetery they moved, stoic before dignitaries from all over the world who had come to honor the dead. This would be what Jack wanted.

He is not dead, though, he never will be dead. Those works for the common good which he set in motion will go on and on. . . . Besides, of course, there is another beginning.

BIBLIOGRAPHY

BURNS, JAMES MACGREGOR. *John Kennedy, A Political Profile.* New York: Harcourt, Brace & Co., 1959, 1960.

DINNEEN, JOSEPH. *The Kennedy Family.* Boston: Little, Brown and Co., 1959.

KENNEDY, JOHN F. *Profiles in Courage.* New York: Harper & Bros., 1956.

LEE, BRUCE. *Boy's Life of John F. Kennedy.* New York: Bold Face Books, Inc., 1961, 1964.

LOWE, JACQUES. *Portrait: The Emergence of John F. Kennedy.* New York: McGraw-Hill Book Co., 1961.

McCARTHY, JOE. *The Remarkable Kennedys.* New York: Dial Press, 1960.

SCHOOR, GENE. *Young John Kennedy.* New York: Harcourt, Brace & World, 1963.

TREGASKIS, RICHARD: *John F. Kennedy and PT-109.* New York: Random House, 1962.

WHO'S WHO IN AMERICA

CURRENT BIOGRAPHY

THE NEW YORK TIMES

INDEX

Finland, invaded by Russia, 90

Fitzgerald, John F. ("Honey Fitz"), 13-18, 19, 137; mission to South America, 65-8, 128; in retirement, 140; aids JFK in politics, 140, 142-3

Fore River Shipyard, Quincy, Mass., 12, 17

Forrestal, James, 101

France, fall of, 88, 89

Germany: submarine warfare (1917), 11-12; i n v a d e s Czechoslovakia (1939), 77; JFK in (1939), 82; in World War II, 83 ff.

Glasgow, Scotland, JFK in, 83-5

Great Britain: Joseph Kennedy as ambassador to, 75 ff., 89 ff.; planned German invasion of, 79; unpreparedness for war, 87-8; German bombings of, 90, 120-1

Haile Selassie, 80

Halsey, Admiral William F., 114

Harris (member crew, PT boat), 104

Hartington, Marchioness of. *See* Kennedy, Kathleen

Hartington, Marquess of. *See* Cavendish, John Robert

Harvard University: Joseph Kennedy, Sr. and, 24; Joseph Kennedy, Jr., at, 40, 70, 72-4, 91; football team, 70, 71; JFK at, 71 ff., 85-8

Harvard Crimson, student paper, 76-7

Hasty Pudding Club, Harvard, 77

Hayden-Stone Company, 13

Hersey, John, 144

Hiroshima, bombing of, 133

Hitler, Adolf, 78, 79, 83, 85, 90, 93-4

Holcombe, Professor Arthur, 24, 86

Holland, invaded by Germans, 79, 88

Horton, Ralph, Jr. ("Rip"), 38 ff., 47 ff., 53-6, 59-60, 69, 71

Hyannis Port, Kennedy home at, 45, 47 ff., 91-6, 117 ff.

International News Service, 134-6

Ireland, JFK visit to, 177

Italy, in World War II, 89

Japan, in World War II, 98, 100, 102 ff.

Jerusalem, JFK in, 81

John XXIII, Pope, 178

Johnson, Lyndon, 168, 180

Johnson, William, 146

Kefauver, Estes, 163

Kennedy, Caroline, 164, 177, 181, 182

Kennedy, Edward, 33, 56, 92, 127-8

Kennedy, Eunice (Mrs. Sargent Shriver), 8, 29; at Hyannis Port, 50 ff., 93, 94; in London, 77, 80; aids JFK in

ABOUT THE AUTHOR

FLORA STROUSSE was born in Baltimore, Maryland, and attended the Maryland Institute, a fine arts school there. After her marriage, she moved to Philadelphia, where she has resided ever since. While raising her two children, she took courses in psychology at the University of Pennsylvania, and English and creative writing "at every possible place," including Temple University and the Bread Loaf Writers' Conference.

These various studies resulted in many diverse editorial posts and a sizable literary output. A secondary interest in medicine led her to edit a paper for the Department of Disease Prevention at the Children's Hospital and to contribute stories and articles to *Hygeia* and *The Journal of Medical Science*. She has published stories in many literary magazines, and one of these stories was included in *All Manner of Men*, the collection of representative fiction edited by Riley Hughes. Her several books for young readers include *The Friar and the Knight* and *Margaret Haughery: The Breadwoman of New Orleans* (both American Background Books), *The Littlest Christmas Tree*, and *John Milton*.

Mrs. Strousse also has worked in the editorial departments of Holt, Rinehart and Winston, and J. B. Lippincott. She has taught creative writing at the Junto Adult School in Philadelphia, and through her personal interest and expert advice has guided numerous young people to successful literary careers.

AMERICAN BACKGROUND BOOKS

*Lives of Catholic Heroes and Heroines
in American History*

AMERICAN BACKGROUND BOOKS is a splendid series for readers ten to fourteen dealing with the lives of Catholic men and women who have played an important role in the history of our Continent. Although most of them concern those whose contributions were made to the discovery, exploration and development of the United States, the series also introduces to boys and girls the heroes and heroines of Canada and other countries of North America. Great explorers, colonizers, war heroes, pioneer women, missionaries as well as those prominent in the fields of art or sport are among those whose lives and adventures light up the pages of these books.

AMERICAN BACKGROUND BOOKS have been written by fine writers eminently qualified to deal with each period and subject. Without departing from the facts, they handle the material in a way that stresses human interest and adventure. These books will foster pride in the American and Catholic heritage and make more vivid some of the most dramatic and exciting episodes in American history.